CDPSE: FOCUSED PREPARATION

Introduction

This focused exam preparation book for the Certified Data Privacy Solutions Engineer (CDPSE) certification is just that, a preparation book. Reading this and completing the prep exam within the book will not guarantee a 'pass' on the exam. This book will provide you with an understanding of how the exam will be presented with similar focus on questions that may be presented to you on the actual exam.

The questions and scenarios within this book are not and will not be the questions you are asked on your exam. The questions within the book are to expand your focus on areas that may not be the actual question posed on the exam.

Your understanding of the question or a particular regulatory requirement will assist your overall preparation in not only knowing a term or a solution, but what might require that solution to be implemented based on a requirement.

The questions and scenarios are based on the publicly available information from the most current common body of knowledge and blueprints for ease of understanding and to supplement your preparation.

This book is structured to ask the same number of questions per topic based on the most current published common body of knowledge.

This book outlines and walks you through one proven and recommended way of preparing for your exam.

Exam Taking Tips

The primary essence of dissecting any exam question is to understand the question being asked.

What is 'it' that the question is asking you?

You have to understand what the question is asking before you can correctly answer the question.

Review and understand the eight domains within the body of knowledge, along with each sub domain, objectives and modules.

Knowing the domains and their objectives will assist you in being able to recall the correct answer for the question.

This book will assist you in determining what the question is asking you to answer.

CDPSE: FOCUSED PREPARATION

Most questions on the exam have one or multiple terms presented to you.

An example of a term may be 'Accountability.' Knowing what that definition is and where in the domain(s) it is relevant, will help you determine the correct answer, if the question is asking you about 'Accountability.'

An example question (bonus question for you, the reader) may be:

Which is an example of direct marketing? (stem)

A. an email sent to an individual about an order she has placed for a book
B. an email sent to an individual promoting a new book which is on sale
C. a letter addressed to 'the household' about a charity bookstore
D. an advertisement on a website promoting a new book which is on sale

The correct answer is B. An email sent to an individual promoting a new pharmaceutical drug which is on sale, is an example of direct marketing. The term 'direct marketing' refers specifically to the communication, by whatever means, of any advertising or marketing material directed to particular individuals. This means that data protection laws apply to the sending of marketing messages only where individuals' personal data is processed in order to communicate the marketing message to them.

Marketing that does not entail processing of any personal data and is therefore not directed at individuals (for example, untargeted website banner advertisements), is not subject to data protection compliance. In addition, messages that are purely service related in nature (messages sent to individuals to inform them, for example, about the status of an order they have placed) do not generally constitute direct marketing.

If your organization resides within the EU and EEA, the GDPR provides the data subject the right to object to processing for the purposes of direct marketing.

See GDPR Recitals 47 and 70, GDPR Article 21, and Article 29 Working Party Opinion 5/2004.

These types of questions, with that thought process, are highly likely to be presented to you on your exam. Understanding those particular requirements and what is recommended as a privacy solution to be implemented is what we focus on here in this book.

The Exam Itself.

The CDPSE certification exam consists of 150 multiple choice questions that cover the exam content outline created from the most recent exam content analysis, depicted below.

You have up to 4 hours (240 minutes) to complete the exam.

CDPSE: FOCUSED PREPARATION

This book provides the similar number of questions based on the following weighted percentages of each domain:

Domain 1: Privacy Governance (34%)
- Governance
    - Personal Data and Information
    - Privacy Laws and Standards across Jurisdictions
    - Privacy Documentation (e.g., Policies, Guidelines)
    - Legal Purpose, Consent, and Legitimate Interest
    - Data Subject Rights
- Management
    - Roles and Responsibilities related to Data
    - Privacy Training and Awareness
    - Vendor and Third-Party Management
    - Audit Process
    - Privacy Incident Management
- Risk Management
    - Risk Management Process
    - Privacy Impact Assessment (PIA)
    - Threats, Attacks, and Vulnerabilities related to Privacy

Domain 2: Privacy Architecture (36%)
- Infrastructure
    - Technology Stacks
    - Cloud-based Services
    - Endpoints
    - Remote Access
    - System Hardening
- Applications and Software
    - Secure Development Lifecycle (e.g., Privacy by Design)
    - Applications and Software Hardening
    - APIs and Services
    - Tracking Technologies
- Technical Privacy Controls
    - Communication and Transport Protocols
    - Encryption, Hashing, and De-identification
    - Key Management
    - Monitoring and Logging
    - Identity and Access Management

Domain 3: Data Cycle (30%)
- Data Purpose
    - Data Inventory and Classification (e.g., Tagging, Tracking, SOR)
    - Data Quality and Accuracy

CDPSE: FOCUSED PREPARATION

- o Dataflow and Usage Diagrams
- o Data Use Limitation
- o Data Analytics (e.g., Aggregation, AI, Machine Learning, Big Data)
- Data Persistence
    - o Data Minimization (e.g., De-identification, Anonymization)
    - o Data Migration
    - o Data Storage
    - o Data Warehousing (e.g., Data Lake)
    - o Data Retention and Archiving
    - o Data Destruction

Reading the questions twice will help you truly understand the question being asked.

If you read the question and know the answer before you look below to the presented answers, trust that intuition. Look at the presented answers to confirm the correct answer.

If your answer is not presented in the answers, look for a similar answer. That 'similar' answer may be your correct answer.

If neither of those answers are presented, re-read the question. Look for the key 'term' and see if there is a word, such as 'any' or 'all' or if the question is asking you for 'what is NOT' a part of the term or question. Those keywords will help you identify possible distracting, presented answers and lead you to eliminate those from the equation of possible questions.

You will then have two good or best answers to select from once you have completed that process.

Reflect on the definitions and terms that you have studied along with your experience to decipher the correct response. Mark that question and move on to the next question.

Learn the terms and definitions, please!

The terms and definitions make up a large portion of the overall content. Utilize those in your day-to-day responsibilities from the point you start preparing for your exam. That will reinforce the terms, their definitions and potentially also prepare you for your future exams.

FINAL PREP

The first time you read the exam question is to train your mind to quickly reflect on the key words you read and what is being asked.

Reading a question twice will highlight those keywords and begin to clarify what the question is really asking you to answer.

CDPSE: FOCUSED PREPARATION

Reflect on those keywords. Terms. Definitions.

Ask yourself what the question is asking you to know.

The first few questions of this book will start you on that process of asking you to read the question twice.

After that, highlight the keywords of the question.

Finally, ask yourself what the question is asking you to know.

Review the questions and choose the correct answer.

Remember, you can flag a question and come back to review it at the end. Do not get frustrated if you don't know the answer.

Don't spend too much time on one particular question. If you are unsure of the answer, flag it, and move on to the next and review ALL flagged items at the end.

Do NOT leave any questions blank or unanswered.

You can also find in our library the CIPM: FOCUSED PREPARATION; the CIPP/US: FOCUSED PREPARATION; the CIPP/E: FOCUSED PREPARATION: and the HCISPP: FOCUSED PREPARATION prep exam books for your use in future exams.

Take your time, prepare as best you can, reference as many resources that you need to feel comfortable and prepared to take the exam.

Now, let's get started with your CDPSE: FOCUSED PREPARATION and thank you for purchasing this book!

Let's give it a go.

CDPSE: FOCUSED PREPARATION

Question 1.

Technologies that enable and enhance and preserve privacy and security of data throughout its entire lifecycle while protecting information privacy by eliminating or minimizing personal data is called?

Technologies that enable and enhance and preserve privacy and security of data throughout its entire lifecycle while protecting information privacy by eliminating or minimizing personal data is called?

Key words: Technologies; preserve privacy; data; lifecycle; information privacy; eliminating; minimizing personal data

Questions to ask yourself – What technologies preserve privacy/data?; What is information lifecycle (term)? What does minimizing personal data mean?

Answers:

A. Confidentiality
B. Data Protection
C. Information Security
D. Privacy Enabling Technologies

CDPSE: FOCUSED PREPARATION

Question 2.

The privacy framework for transpacific exchanges of personal data between Asia-Pacific and the United States is called?

The <u>privacy framework</u> for <u>transpacific exchanges</u> of <u>personal data</u> between <u>Asia-Pacific</u> and the <u>United States</u> is called?

Key words: privacy framework; transpacific exchanges; personal data; Asia-Pacific; United States

Questions to ask yourself – What is a privacy framework? What framework applies to transpacific personal data exchanges? What framework applies to Asia Pacific and the United States?

Answers:

A. General Data Protection Regulation
B. Privacy Shield
C. Organization for Economic Co-operation and Development Transborder Flow
D. Asia-Pacific Economic Cooperation (APEC) Privacy Framework

CDPSE: FOCUSED PREPARATION

Question 3.

The right of a human individual to control the distribution of information about him or herself is called?

The <u>right</u> of a human individual to <u>control</u> the <u>distribution</u> of <u>information</u> about him or herself is called?

Key words: right; control; distribution; information

Questions to ask yourself – What is a right of a human?; What control do I have of my information? Who do I want to have my information?

Answers:

A. Confidentiality
B. Data Protection
C. Information Security
D. Privacy

CDPSE: FOCUSED PREPARATION

Question 4.

On July 16, 2020, the European Union Court of Justice (CJEU) invalidated the EU-US Privacy Shield in its decision in Facebook Ireland v. Schrems (Schrems II). The court determined that the Privacy Shield transfer mechanism does not comply with the level of protection required under EU law.
The decision reinforces the European Union's commitment to protecting what?

On July 16, 2020, the <u>European Union Court of Justice (CJEU)</u> <u>invalidated</u> the <u>EU-US Privacy Shield</u> in its decision in Facebook Ireland v. Schrems (Schrems II). The court determined that the Privacy Shield <u>transfer mechanism</u> does <u>not comply</u> with the <u>level of protection</u> required under EU law.
The decision reinforces the European Union's commitment to protecting what?

Key words: European Union Court of Justice; invalidated; EU-US Privacy Shield; transfer mechanism; not comply; level of protection

Questions to ask yourself – What is being transferred? What did the EU-US Privacy Shield provide organizations?

Answers:

A. Regulations
B. Security
C. Privacy
D. Citizens

CDPSE: FOCUSED PREPARATION

Question 5.

Defense in Depth (DiD) models allow your organization to apply several layers (depth) of controls across its perimeter to protect the organization's assets.
The DiD model promotes the possible breach of multiple, exterior depth controls before being detected and responded to.
One key access control that, if implemented, will protect your core assets is the?

Answers:

A. Principle of Least Privilege (PoLP)
B. Trust Model
C. Security Guard
D. Training and Awareness

CDPSE: FOCUSED PREPARATION

Question 6.

You are the privacy solutions engineer professional within your multinational organization and are reviewing proposed new technologies being requested for implementation within your facilities. You conduct an analysis of how information is handled, ensuring that the handling is in compliance with legal, regulatory and policy requirements regarding privacy that your organization is accountable to and for.

What is this analysis?

Answers:

A. Privacy Notice
B. Privacy Impact Assessment
C. Data Protection Impact Assessment
D. Privacy Audit

CDPSE: FOCUSED PREPARATION

Question 7.

Your organization recently conducted its semi-annually risk assessment. Throughout the assessment, multiple findings were identified, verified with different responses.

The reason your organization conducts a semi-annual assessment is due to the following that constitute risk assessment factors: Number of breaches; number of outages; unauthorized access; lost assets; software viruses; investigations.

Multiple risks identified were dodged. Numerous risks were agreed on. Others were alleviated and others are protected by a cyber insurance program.

What is the last action called from the risk response strategies?

Answers:

A. Avoidance
B. Acceptance
C. Mitigation
D. Transfer

CDPSE: FOCUSED PREPARATION

Question 8.

The National Institute of Standards and Technology (NIST) developed a six-step process for the Risk Management Framework (RMF), and one of those 6 steps helps management to review business processes 24/7 to see if the performance, effectiveness and efficiency are achieving the anticipated targets, or if there is something deviating from the intended targets.

Your multinational organization utilizes the RMF along with a formal process of defining its IT systems, categorizing each of these systems by the level of risk, application of the controls, continuous monitoring of the applied controls, and the assessment of the effectiveness of these controls against security threats.

What is this process named?

Answers:

A. Continuous Control Monitoring
B. Continuous Monitoring
C. Program Management
D. Risk Assessment Process

CDPSE: FOCUSED PREPARATION

Question 9.

You are the privacy solutions engineer of your multinational organization and have conducted your data inventory exercise. You are now in the process of implementing a roadmap that provides the structure or checklists (documented privacy procedures and processes) to guide the privacy solutions engineer through privacy management and prompts them for the details to determine all privacy-relevant decisions for the organization.

This process is a certifiable framework that provides organizations with a comprehensive, flexible, and an efficient approach to regulatory compliance and risk management and ties into processes and programs. What is this process called?

Answers:

A. Privacy Program Framework (PPM)
B. HITRUST Cybersecurity Framework (CSF)
C. NIST Cybersecurity Framework (CSF)
D. NIST Privacy Framework (PF)

CDPSE: FOCUSED PREPARATION

Question 10.

Your pharmaceutical organization has continued to grow and mature its overall privacy and security posture.
You are reviewing all current privacy and security policies for any gaps based on your regulatory mapping and data flow paths that have been documented.
The security team is overlaying their security controls along the data flow path, both internally and externally.
You are continuing to review all contracts where sensitive information is being shared or disclosed and updating requirements for both privacy and security measures to be applied.
As you review all controls in place and strategically planned to be implemented, your privacy and security teams have controls that support identifying, protecting, detecting, responding, and recovering controls across your entire organization.
Which framework have you implemented?

Answers:

A. Privacy Program Framework (PPM)
B. HITRUST Cybersecurity Framework (CSF)
C. NIST Cybersecurity Framework (CSF)
D. NIST Privacy Framework (PF)

CDPSE: FOCUSED PREPARATION

Question 11.

Your multinational healthcare organization is preparing to share ePHI with multiple processors. You are reviewing Article 4(5) of the GDPR for guidance.

What is the processing of protected personal data in such a manner that the personal data can no longer be attributed to a specific data subject without the use of additional information, provided that such additional information is kept separately and is subject to technical and organizational measures to ensure that the personal data are not attributed to an identified or identifiable natural person?

Answers:

A. Cleansed
B. Disposed
C. Encrypted
D. Pseudonymized

CDPSE: FOCUSED PREPARATION

Question 12.

Your multinational healthcare organization is conducting cross-border transfers of electronic protected health information from multiple Asia-Pacific regions to other regions.

Your cross-border transfer program framework consists of all of the following within the Asia-Pacific (APEC) Privacy Framework objectives, except the following:

Answers:

A. To prevent harm
B. To limit collection
C. To provide choice
D. To encrypt data

CDPSE: FOCUSED PREPARATION

Question 13.

General Data Protection Law (LGPD) is Brazil's first comprehensive data protection law and is designed to enhance the privacy and protection of personal data of individuals in Brazil. The LGPD heavily resembles the EU General Data Protection Regulation (GDPR).

On September 17, 2020, the Brazilian president approved the bill, resulting in the LGPD taking effect on September 18, 2020.

At the end of October 2020, India announced that they are currently working towards a privacy regulation, similar, yet possibly more stringent than GDPR? What will this new law be named?

Answers:

A. General Data Protection Regulation (GDPR)
B. Personal Data Protection Act (PDPA)
C. Privacy Data Protection Act (PrDPA)
D. Personal Privacy Rights Act (PPRA)

CDPSE: FOCUSED PREPARATION

Question 14.

You are the privacy solutions engineer within your U.S. domiciled healthcare organization. You have been reviewing the Department of Health and Human Services (HHS) website for recent fines and penalties levied against other organizations to determine if your organization has similar risks.
You have reviewed multiple complaints that have been submitted to your organization based on different components and protocols.
You know that if the OCR accepts a complaint for investigation, the OCR will notify the person who filed the complaint and the covered entity named in it. Then the complainant and the covered entity are asked to present information about the incident or problem described in the complaint.
The OCR may request specific information from each to get an understanding of the facts. Covered entities are required by law to cooperate with complaint investigations.
The OCR reviews the information, or evidence, that it gathers in each case. In some cases, it may determine that the covered entity did not violate the requirements of the Privacy or Security Rule. If the evidence indicates that the covered entity was not in compliance, OCR will attempt to resolve the case with the covered entity by obtaining each of these except:

Answers:

A. Voluntary compliance
B. Corrective action
C. Resolution agreement
D. Consent decree

CDPSE: FOCUSED PREPARATION

Question 15.

You are the privacy solutions engineer for a small retail organization that is conducting a self-regulatory self-assessment questionnaire (SAQ). Which one of these would this report best support?

Answers:

A. GDPR
B. EU Directive on Electronic Commerce
C. PCI DSS
D. U.S. HIPAA

CDPSE: FOCUSED PREPARATION

Question 16.

You are the privacy solutions engineer working for a multinational healthcare organization. You are drafting a statement that is a public document which identifies who the data controller is, with contact details for its Data Protection Officer. It should also explain the purposes for which protected personal health data are collected and used, how the data are used and disclosed, how long it is kept, and the controller's legal basis for processing.
What is this statement named?

Answers:

A. Privacy Statement
B. Privacy Policy
C. Privacy Notice
D. GDPR Notice

CDPSE: FOCUSED PREPARATION

Question 17.

Your organization is a covered entity accountable to being compliant with HIPAA and your medical staff has access to all medical records within your organization. Each staff member is trained frequently on proper handling, access, and protecting of sensitive data. If one of your medical practitioners accesses an medical record in which they are not providing care to the individual associated with the record, which HIPAA rule has been violated?

Answers:

A. HITECH
B. Privacy Rule
C. Security Rule
D. Enforcement Rule

CDPSE: FOCUSED PREPARATION

Question 18.

In 2009, the American Recovery and Reinvestment Act (ARRA) was signed into law by President Barack Obama. Prior to this Act, approximately only 10% of hospitals had adopted electronic health records. In order to advance healthcare, improve efficiencies and care coordination while making it easier for health information to be shared between different covered entities, electronic health records needed to be adopted.
A subsequent Act was introduced and signed into law under the ARRA to promote and expand the adoption of health information. What Act is this?

Answers:

A. Health Insurance Portability and Accountability Act
B. Health Information Exchange
C. Health Information Technology for Economic and Clinical Health Act
D. Medicare Merit-Based Incentive Program

CDPSE: FOCUSED PREPARATION

Question 19.

You are the privacy practitioner for an European organization. You are new to the position and are evaluating the best compliance framework that may propose to implement within your organization.
Ensuring the framework is current and applicable, you review current and past frameworks for validity, knowledge, and efficiencies.
In which chronological order were the following frameworks adopted?

Answers:

A. Directive on Privacy and Electronic Communications/Data Protection Directive/Directive on Electronic Commerce/GDPR
B. Data Protection Directive/Directive on Privacy and Electronic Communications/Directive on Electronic Commerce/GDPR
C. GDPR/Directive on Privacy and Electronic Communications/Data Protection Directive/Directive on Electronic Commerce
D. Council 108/Data Protection Directive/Directive on Electronic Commerce/Directive on Privacy and Electronic Communications

CDPSE: FOCUSED PREPARATION

Question 20.

In order for you to assess a cloud provider, you must understand the cloud provider's?

Answers:

A. Privacy
B. Mission Statement
C. Notice
D. Policies

CDPSE: FOCUSED PREPARATION

Question 21.

Your organization is domiciled in the European Union (EU).
The third-party management program is reviewing and assessing prospective vendors to outsource certain data processing activities.
What is one topic that is not a priority for you to assess?

Answers:

A. Appropriate technical and organizational measures
B. Processor shall not engage another processor without specific or general written authorization
C. Processing by a processor shall be governed by a contract
D. What data the processor will process

CDPSE: FOCUSED PREPARATION

Question 22.

As you and your organization review and assess prospective vendors/processors, you review data sharing implications, adequacy decisions, data subject's rights and appropriate technical and organizational measures.
Which of the following are not privacy matters to consider?

Answers:

A. Geographical location
B. Global Privacy Regulations
C. Cross-border data sharing
D. Competitor's Privacy Strategy

CDPSE: FOCUSED PREPARATION

Question 23.

You are the privacy solutions engineer for a U.S. based organization and are seeking new staff members for open positions. Your organization has contracted with an outside agency to collect credit reports on all applicants.
That particular vendor must provide your organization with all of the documents collected on the applicants and attest that they have provided all documents and destroyed any copies of data they collected.
Your organization has implemented a data retention policy. Based on the information provided by the Credit Reporting Agency (CRA) to your organization, your organization decides not to hire one particular individual.
After the individual discovers they were not hired due to the inaccurate information provided to the hiring organization, they may file a complaint with which agency?

Answers:

A. FCC
B. FTC
C. FDCPA
D. SNPRM

CDPSE: FOCUSED PREPARATION

Question 24.

A vendor is being assessed for future business operations and relations with your organization. Your organization will be sharing sensitive information to be processed by this vendor.
You are reviewing their information risk management model and incident response plans. Your organization is required to report a known data breach within 72 hours to its regulators, however, the vendor currently reports any known data breaches within 30 days.

What type of instrument should be utilized in order to contract with this particular vendor to ensure they are compliant with your requirements?

Answers:

A. Business Associate Agreement (BAA)
B. SLA
C. MTTR
D. Legal Liability

CDPSE: FOCUSED PREPARATION

Question 25.

As you assess your prospective vendors, what is one topic that is not a priority for you to assess?

Answers:

A. Financial
B. Geographic Location(s)
C. Privacy Framework
D. Data Inventory

CDPSE: FOCUSED PREPARATION

Question 26.

Your organization is a covered entity and has suffered a data breach. The Office of Civil Rights has been investigating the breach and has determined your organization had a duty to your patients in protecting their data and that duty along with the data was breached, which has now caused harm or injury to your patients. What is this called?

Answers:

A. Due Care
B. Due Diligence
C. Negligence
D. Contract Law

CDPSE: FOCUSED PREPARATION

Question 27.

Your organization is domiciled in New Mexico. Your organization encrypts and redacts the personal and business critical data. Your organization suffers a data breach. After you have contacted your data breach coach and deploy a forensic investigator, it is determined that your encryption key has been compromised. Which law must you comply with and notify compromised data subjects?

Answers:

A. HIPAA
B. Nevada HB 15
C. New Mexico HB 15
D. New Mexico Privacy Protection Act

CDPSE: FOCUSED PREPARATION

Question 28.

Your organization is domiciled in Tennessee. Your organization encrypts and redacts the personal and business critical data. Your organization suffers a data breach. After you have contacted your data breach coach and deploy a forensic investigator, it is determined that your encryption key has not been compromised. Based on your which statutory requirement will you reference to determine whether or not you must notify impacted Tennessee residents?

Answers:

A. Tennessee HB 2005
B. Tennessee SB 2005
C. Tennessee SB 2015
D. Tennessee HB 2015

CDPSE: FOCUSED PREPARATION

Question 29.

Your organization has suffered a data breach within your archived information. What policy will be looked at to determine whether or not your organization has complied with that policy?

Answers:

A. Acceptable Use
B. BYOD
C. Incident Response Plan
D. Retention

CDPSE: FOCUSED PREPARATION

Question 30.

You are the privacy solutions engineer within your organization and are protecting the infrastructure of your organization.

With that, your teams are cleaning up programs, utilizing service packs, applying patches in accordance with your patch management program, implementing and applying group policies within the security templates, and following and updating configuration baselines.

What is your team executing?

Answers:

A. Technology review
B. System hardening
C. Security protocols
D. Secure development

CDPSE: FOCUSED PREPARATION

Question 31.

In today's connected world, software application resiliency takes an increasingly predominant role. With the continuous discovery of new vulnerabilities in more connected systems and sensors, customers need software systems to be secure, safe, and reliable.

All of your software inventory, including new software, legacy software, open source, and/or 3rd-party software, must be protected to minimize risks of security breaches, data loss, and more.

This protective measure is done through three core techniques: software vulnerability analysis, binary patching and transformation, and software monitoring.

What is this called?

Answers:

A. System hardening
B. Application hardening
C. Software hardening
D. Threat modeling

CDPSE: FOCUSED PREPARATION

Question 32.

This infrastructure protection measure is a collection of tools, techniques, and best practices to reduce vulnerability in technology applications, systems, infrastructure, firmware, and other areas.

The goal of this action is to reduce security risk by eliminating potential attack vectors and condensing the system's attack surface. By removing superfluous programs, accounts functions, applications, ports, permissions, access, etc. attackers and malware have fewer opportunities to gain a foothold within your IT ecosystem.

What is this called?

Answers:

A. Application hardening
B. Operating system hardening
C. Server hardening
D. System hardening

CDPSE: FOCUSED PREPARATION

Question 33.

Data privacy is a part of the data protection area that deals with the proper handling of data. This includes how data should be collected, stored and shared with any third parties, as well as compliance with the applicable privacy laws.
Data privacy is more about properly utilizing data while protecting the privacy preferences of individuals.
Data privacy is not one of these. Which one?
Answers:

A. Relationship between data collected and the individual who provided the data and the data owner
B. Public expectation of privacy
C. Is not blocking data and disposing it without use
D. Regulatory requirements to protect data

CDPSE: FOCUSED PREPARATION

Question 34.

Access to data and devices is limited to authorized individuals, processes, and devices, and is managed consistent with the assessed risk of unauthorized access falls under which NIST Privacy Framework core function?

Answers:

A. Protect
B. Control
C. Detect
D. Identify

CDPSE: FOCUSED PREPARATION

Question 35.

Technical security solutions are managed to ensure the security and resilience of systems/products/services and associated data, consistent with related policies, processes, procedures, and agreements fall within which NIST Privacy Framework core function?
Answers:

A. Identify
B. Detect
C. Control
D. Protect

CDPSE: FOCUSED PREPARATION

Question 36.

You are working with procurement and legal on contracts with suppliers and third-party partners that are used to implement appropriate measures designed to meet the objectives of your organization's cybersecurity program and Cyber Supply Chain Risk Management Plan.

Which NIST framework function are you referencing for this task?

Answers:

A. Identify
B. Protect
C. Detect
D. Control

CDPSE: FOCUSED PREPARATION

Question 37.

Access permissions and authorizations are managed, incorporating the principles of least privilege and separation of duties is part of which domain of the CDPSE outline?

Answers:

A. Privacy Governance
B. Data Cycle
C. Privacy Architecture
D. Privacy Cycle

CDPSE: FOCUSED PREPARATION

Question 38.

To build this process within your organization, you as the privacy solutions engineer will need a proactive and continuous approach to both privacy and cyber risk management.

This process includes embedding risk management within all business processes where customers, partners, and third-party vendors are made full-time stakeholders in your organization's process, while the business is made fully aware of all cyber risks to make better business decisions.

Answers:

A. Accountability
B. Resilience
C. Response
D. Identification

CDPSE: FOCUSED PREPARATION

Question 39.

There are many steps and proactive measures to develop and create a cyber resilient organization. There are prioritized actions to start the resiliency program. Which one would you start with?

Answers:

A. Automation
B. Quantification
C. Security by design
D. Zero trust model

CDPSE: FOCUSED PREPARATION

Question 40.

Your organization's privileged users, third-party stakeholders, senior executives and physical and cybersecurity personnel understand their roles and responsibilities due to table-top exercises and annual policy reviews.

What category do these actions fall within the Protect function under the NIST CSF?

Answers:

A. Identify
B. Data Security
C. Awareness and Training
D. Information Protection Processes and Procedures

CDPSE: FOCUSED PREPARATION

Question 41.

Your organization suffered a data breach, which your incident response team was able to identify, contain and respond in a timely fashion to limit the negative impact on the organization.

You are now in the recovery aspect (5th core function of the NIST CSF) and following your recovery processes and procedures are being executed and maintained to ensure restoration of systems or assets affected by the cybersecurity event.

What is your first step of the recovery process?

Answers:

A. Incorporate lessons learned
B. Update recovery strategies
C. Follow the recovery plan
D. Manage public relations and expectations

CDPSE: FOCUSED PREPARATION

Question 42.

Restoration activities are coordinated with internal and external parties (e.g., coordinating centers, Internet Service Providers, owners of attacking systems, victims, other CSIRTs, and vendors).

Which NIST core function would this fall under?

Answers:

A. Recover
B. Respond
C. Communicate
D. Governance

CDPSE: FOCUSED PREPARATION

Question 43.

Identifying everyone residing in a country, especially the poor, is an indispensable part of pursuing universal health coverage (UHC).

Some countries, such as South Korea and Thailand use this as their unique health identifier.

What is this called?

Answers:

A. National unique identification number
B. National health identification number
C. National unique health identification number
D. Civil registration

CDPSE: FOCUSED PREPARATION

Question 44.

You, as the privacy solutions engineer, are designing the best practices to implement within your privacy and cyber security programs.

You are enforcing least privilege access of users, conducting continuous scans, enforcing system hardening, enforcing application controls, and deploying a SIEM solution, on top of other proactive preventative measures.

What type of security are you addressing with these programs?

Answers:

A. Application security
B. Endpoint security
C. Software hardening
D. Incident response planning

CDPSE: FOCUSED PREPARATION

Question 45.

You are migrating data from legacy systems to modernize your information systems. Your analysis has determined that your current information systems were never designed to quickly adapt to changing business dynamics or to address your customer's expectations.

As you develop your business case for the data migration strategy and required resources, you have determined all of the following are critical risks to address in the business case development, except?

Answers:

A. Depreciated data values
B. Security
C. Vendor solutions
D. Roll back strategy

CDPSE: FOCUSED PREPARATION

Question 46.

As the increase in ransomware attacks (+700% since March 2020) continue to impact businesses around the world, key administrative and technical risks have been identified that are connected to those attacks being successful.

Having RDP enabled without other compensating controls in place; the lack of MFA implemented across the organization; the lack of EDR solutions and what other lacking control is a key contributor to ransomware attacks?

Answers:

A. Encryption
B. Privacy and Security Training and Awareness
C. HR Controls
D. Communications

CDPSE: FOCUSED PREPARATION

Question 47.

Clinical trials can have a profound impact on millions of people, but the decision to join is a very personal one. If you decide to choose to participate, you will be provided the details of the study, including possible risks and benefits, so you'll know what to expect. If you decide to participate, you'll give written permission for additional screenings and access to your health records.

What is this called when you decide to participate at this point?

Answers:

A. Written consent
B. Informed consent
C. Unambiguous consent
D. Authorization

CDPSE: FOCUSED PREPARATION

Question 48.

In December 2020, a major state-sponsored attack broke into FireEye's network and stole the company's Red Team penetration testing tools.

A few days after the announcement, a breach investigation discovered that SolarWinds Orion updates had been corrupted and weaponized by hackers.

As part of the investigation and mitigation recommendations, a key malicious domain name used in the attack had been commandeered by security experts and used as a "killswitch."

What is the definition of a "killswitch" In this situation?

Answers:

A. ...are designed to prevent your connection from accidental exposure
B. ...is a security feature that allows a data owner to remotely render a system inoperable
C. ...that the domain was reconfigured to act as a 'killswitch' that would prevent the malware from continuing to operate
D. ...is used to completely shut off a device or system

Question 49.

Cloud environments experience the same level and number of threats as do traditional data center environments. Cloud computing runs software, software has vulnerabilities, and adversaries try to exploit those vulnerabilities.

Cloud computing, responsibility for mitigating the risks that result from these software vulnerabilities is shared between the CSP and the cloud consumer.

As a result, consumers must understand the division of responsibilities and trust that the CSP meets their responsibilities. The following list of cloud-unique and shared cloud/on-premise vulnerabilities and threats were identified. Which is not a cloud-based risk?

Answers:

A. Reduced consumer visibility and control
B. On-demand self-service
C. APIs cannot be compromised
D. Unauthorized use/access

CDPSE: FOCUSED PREPARATION

Question 50.

Which of the following is a method used to prevent SQL injection attacks?

Answers:

A. Utilizing data compression
B. Utilizing data classification
C. Utilizing parameterized database queries
D. Utilizing data warehousing

CDPSE: FOCUSED PREPARATION

Question 51.

A multinational organization has decided to outsource a portion of their Information Technology organization to a third-party provider's facility.

This provider will be responsible for the design, development, testing, and support of several critical, customer- based applications used by the organization.

The third party needs to have?

Answers:

A. Processes that are identical to that of the organization doing the outsourcing
B. Access to the original personnel that were on staff at the organization
C. The ability to maintain all of the applications in languages they are familiar with
D. Access to the skill sets consistent with the programming languages used by the organization

CDPSE: FOCUSED PREPARATION

Question 52.

Which one of the following is a threat related to the use of web-based client-side input validation?

Answers:

A. The web server would not be able to validate the input after transmission
B. The client system could receive invalid input from the web server
C. Users would be able to alter the input after validation has occurred
D. The web server would not be able to receive invalid input from the client

CDPSE: FOCUSED PREPARATION

Question 53.

Which of the following is a security limitation of File Transfer Protocol (FTP)?

Answers:

A. Authentication is not encrypted
B. Passive FTP is not compatible with web browsers
C. Anonymous access is allowed
D. FTP uses Transmission Control Protocol (TCP) ports 20 and 21

CDPSE: FOCUSED PREPARATION

Question 54.

In Disaster Recovery (DR) and business continuity training, which BEST describes a functional rehearsal?

Answers:

A. A full-scale simulation of an emergency and the subsequent response functions
B. A functional evacuation of personnel
C. An activation of the backup site
D. A specific test by response teams of individual emergency response functions

CDPSE: FOCUSED PREPARATION

Question 55.

A vulnerability in which of the following components would be MOST difficult to detect?

Answers:

A. Kernel
B. Shared libraries
C. Hardware
D. System application

CDPSE: FOCUSED PREPARATION

Question 56.

Which of the following is not a response to a prepared security assessment report that you created with your assessment of your organization's risk posture?

Answers:

A. Transfer of risk
B. Transfer of acceptance of risk
C. Share risk
D. Accept risk

CDPSE: FOCUSED PREPARATION

Question 57.

A Denial of Service (DoS) attack on a syslog server exploits weakness in which of the following protocols?

Answers:

A. Point-to-Point Protocol (PPP) and Internet Control Message Protocol (ICMP)
B. Address Resolution Protocol (ARP) and Reverse Address Resolution Protocol (RARP)
C. Transmission Control Protocol (TCP) and User Datagram Protocol (UDP)
D. Transport Layer Security (TLS) and Secure Sockets Layer (SSL)

CDPSE: FOCUSED PREPARATION

Question 58.

In a data classification scheme, the data is owned by the?

Answers:

A. Business Managers
B. Privacy Officer
C. Legal
D. Users

CDPSE: FOCUSED PREPARATION

Question 59.

Medical records are the document that explains all details about the patient's history, clinical findings, diagnostic test results, pre and postoperative care, patient's progress and medication.

Management of those records is the part of records management that relates to the operation of a healthcare practice. It is the field of management that is responsible for all records throughout their lifecycle from creation, receipt, maintenance, and use to disposal.

As part of this management program, a U.S. based healthcare organization must retain those records for how long?

Answers:

A. 5 years
B. 6 years
C. 7 years
D. 10 years

CDPSE: FOCUSED PREPARATION

Question 60.

HR is reviewing candidate's resumes and background information based on an open job posting. What is one risk area that you, as the privacy solutions engineer, should work with Legal and HR on, as it relates to the background information gathered?

Answers:

A. Data Retention
B. Data Policies
C. Information
D. Training

CDPSE: FOCUSED PREPARATION

Question 61.

Your organization has completed their regulatory mapping exercise and determined and created their data retention policy. The institution has adopted two possible standards for destroying the data, which are degaussing and shredding. What is another way to destroy the data electronically?

Answers:

A. Melt
B. Burn
C. Erase
D. Overwrite

CDPSE: FOCUSED PREPARATION

Question 62.

Your organization, a covered entity within the U.S., has suffered a data breach within your archived information. What policy will be looked at to determine whether or not your organization has complied with that policy?

Answers:

A. Acceptable Use
B. BYOD
C. Incident Response Plan
D. Retention

CDPSE: FOCUSED PREPARATION

Question 63.

A California, U.S. based organization receives its first subject access request (SAR). The privacy officer is alerted to receipt of the request in a timely fashion. What document will be referenced, that was developed in the establishment of the privacy program, that will assist in determining where the SAR's information resides?

Answers:

A. Data Classification Policy
B. Privacy Program Scope
C. Regulatory Map
D. Data Inventory

CDPSE: FOCUSED PREPARATION

Question 64.

A global multi diversified organization located in numerous countries would be best to implement this type of governance model?

Answers:

A. Centralized
B. Distributed
C. Hybrid
D. External

CDPSE: FOCUSED PREPARATION

Question 65.

Your global financial organization is structuring your privacy team. Which privacy domain houses this action item?

Answers:

A. Measure
B. Improve
C. Privacy Program Framework
D. Developing a Privacy Program

CDPSE: FOCUSED PREPARATION

Question 66.

An international organization is implementing their privacy program. While they are in that process, they are conducting self-assessments, developing procedures, communicating and monitoring the program. What type of management is this called?

Answers:

A. Information Security Management System
B. Risk Management
C. Centralized Management
D. Information Management

CDPSE: FOCUSED PREPARATION

Question 67.

As privacy laws and regulations continue to expand and change, complying and monitoring with those changes is critical for your organization's privacy program success. What is one solution that provides organizations with updated changes, monitoring and auditing performances of their processes and procedures?

Answers:

A. Internal Audit
B. Second-party Audit
C. Third-party Audit
D. Third-party Privacy Compliance Platform and Tools

CDPSE: FOCUSED PREPARATION

Question 68.

Prior to a new service or system being implemented in your international organization, this type of action is required to be conducted?

Answers:

A. Data Privacy Impact Assessment
B. Privacy Impact Assessment
C. Privacy Assessment
D. Risk Assessment

CDPSE: FOCUSED PREPARATION

Question 69.

Your organization is capturing and documenting where and what information is flowing, both internally and externally. What is this type of exercise?

Answers:

A. Regulatory Map
B. Legal Map
C. Data Inventory Map
D. Data Map

CDPSE: FOCUSED PREPARATION

Question 70.

What is one risk area that you, as the privacy solutions engineer, should focus on, as it relates to a vendor gathering sensitive information from your organization is what?

Answers:

A. Procurement
B. Vendor Assessment
C. Information Risk
D. Communications

CDPSE: FOCUSED PREPARATION

Question 71.

What must an efficient and successful privacy program within an organization be built with?

Answers:

A. Data Map
B. Regulatory Map
C. Compliance Map
D. Comprehensive View

CDPSE: FOCUSED PREPARATION

Question 72.

Your organization completed the data inventory exercise. Who in your organization determines what classifications of information are arranged into those categories?

Answers:

A. Chief Security Officer
B. Chief Executive Officer
C. Privacy Officer
D. Human Resources

CDPSE: FOCUSED PREPARATION

Question 73.

Your multinational organization is acquiring another multinational organization. As part of the privacy checkpoint, your organization's processes should consist of conducting a _____ prior to the integration of the acquired organization's systems and processes.

Answers:

A. Divestiture
B. Data inventory
C. Regulatory map
D. Risk Assessment

CDPSE: FOCUSED PREPARATION

Question 74.

Your organization is capturing and documenting where and what information is flowing, both internally and externally. What does the end product assist your organization with?

Answers:

A. Identifies vendors
B. Identifies regulatory requirements
C. Identifies classification
D. Identifies personal information use

CDPSE: FOCUSED PREPARATION

Question 75.

One of the goals that is not one of the privacy solution engineer's roles is to?

Answers:

A. To identify their supply chain's privacy risks.
B. To identify their organizations, employees, and customer's risks.
C. To identify current state of policies, procedures, and any supporting documentation.
D. Promote consumer trust.

CDPSE: FOCUSED PREPARATION

Question 76.

Which of the following groups are not a priority group for the development of your privacy policies and procedures within your organization?

Answers:

A. Human Resources
B. Legal
C. Business Development
D. External Audit

CDPSE: FOCUSED PREPARATION

Question 77.

A multinational organization's privacy program maturity level is based on how established the program is functioning in multiple areas. Generally, if your privacy program has recently been created where you are still evaluating and inventorying what the organization has and does not have in place for policies, processes and procedures, the privacy program maturity level is at this stage?

Answers:

A. Repeatable
B. Defined
C. Ad Hoc
D. Managed

CDPSE: FOCUSED PREPARATION

Question 78.

Once the policies, procedures and security controls have been assessed on your potential cloud provider, whom within your organization should approve of this type of vendor?

Answers:

A. General Counsel
B. Privacy Program Manager
C. Chief Information Security Officer
D. Chief Information Officer

CDPSE: FOCUSED PREPARATION

Question 79.

Your multinational organization processes and collects over 1,000,000 credit card transactions annually.
You collect credit card transactions at a kiosk and registration desk for all in-coming patients.
You collect credit card transactions in the café, gift shop, and pharmacy, as well.
You have conducted an assessment on your PCI-DSS compliance. The PCI-DSS deals strictly with payment card data and cardholder information, such as credit/debit card numbers, primary account numbers (PAN), and sensitive authentication data (SAD) such as CVVs and magnetic stripe data, from all the major card schemes.

The GDPR has a much wider scope and covers any personally identifiable information (PII). The type of data in scope for GDPR includes PII related to any EU resident, whether it is connected to his or her private, professional or public life. This can include a name, home address, photo, email address, bank details, medical information, posts on social networking websites, or a computer's IP address.
Your organization suffers a breach that violates PCI DSS compliance, which now, also, violates the GDPR.
Which data protection principle applies here?

Answers:

A. Data minimization
B. Integrity and Confidentiality
C. Storage limitation
D. Purpose limitation

CDPSE: FOCUSED PREPARATION

Question 80.

Your organization is outsourcing its account management program.

When this happens, what type of service are you requesting?

Answers:

A. Platform as a Service (PaaS)
B. Desktop as a Service (DaaS)
C. Identity as a Service (IDaaS)
D. Software as a Service (SaaS)

CDPSE: FOCUSED PREPARATION

Question 81.

An organization that suffers a cyber event may be investigated to determine if they had the appropriate policies and procedures in place, along with documented training for their workforce. If the organization had those correct controls in place, this organization is able to prove that they have?

Answers:

A. Consumer Trust
B. Compliance
C. Accountability
D. Responsibility

CDPSE: FOCUSED PREPARATION

Question 82.

You have set up your data warehouse to be read-only by default. This prevents any dangerous SQL write statements from being executed on your data.

What is this called?

Answers:

A. Slave read-only
B. Data encryption
C. Custom user group development
D. BI tool implementation

CDPSE: FOCUSED PREPARATION

Question 83.

As your organization plans its transition from a data lake to a data warehouse solution, there are a number of proactive preventative steps your organization will need to take into consideration to protect the confidentiality of the data.

Understanding that more groups, more people and possibly more systems will have access to this data, your organization will need to identify what data characteristics are stored in the warehouse, to include PII, financial information, sensitive data, etc.

You need to ensure that sensitive information is aligned to what is being stored, how it's restricted in the data warehouse, and how it can be accessed via your BI tools.

What is the most direct way to limit access to the data?

Answers:

A. Custom user groups
B. Role-based access
C. Slave read-only
D. Enforce rules at database level

CDPSE: FOCUSED PREPARATION

Question 84.

You have implemented Identifying, Governing, Controlling, Communicating, and Protecting functional controls to assist in protecting the privacy of your organization's data.

Which of these functional core controls addresses disassociated processing?

Answers:

A. Identify
B. Control
C. Protect
D. Govern

CDPSE: FOCUSED PREPARATION

Question 85.

Your businesses must know what their Location Based Service (LBS) does, what type of data it collects and whether that data is shared with affiliates, partners or third parties.

A number of critical threats posed to the privacy of individuals stemming from LBS services is the unintended revelation of a user's home address, and websites demonstrating the danger of location-sharing by providing a database of empty homes based on users' "check-ins" elsewhere.

While these may be some of the more extreme examples, it is not uncommon for some LBS-enabled popular services to omit clear disclosures about the extent to which personal information is collected from the consumer and how it is used and have a process that obtains informed consumer consent for such data collection.

How should you conduct threat analysis on LBS services?

A. Conduct threat modeling
B. Vulnerability assessments
C. Conduct location assessments
D. Turn of LBS services

CDPSE: FOCUSED PREPARATION

Question 86.

In this type of threat, the attacker can receive continuous updates of user location in real time, which can be used to identify the user's location routes, predict future locations, and/or frequently traveled routes with sufficient accuracy using a user's mobility patterns.

What type of threat is this called?

Answers:

A. Identification threat
B. Profiling threat
C. Tracking threat
D. Data threat

CDPSE: FOCUSED PREPARATION

Question 87.

Your technology organization is finalizing both the privacy policy and the information security policy. They are both drastically different, to include the structure to how they are presented and available for consumption.

They are both presented in with a layered approach. One of them is defining three levels. The top layer is a high-level document containing the controller's policy statement. The next layer is a more detailed document that sets out the security controls that will be implemented to achieve the policy statements. The third layer is the most detailed and contains the operating procedures, which explain how the policy statements will be achieved in practice.

Which policy are we discussing?

Answers:

A. Privacy Policy
B. Information Security Policy
C. Integrity Policy
D. Privacy Notice (layered)

CDPSE: FOCUSED PREPARATION

Question 88.

A publicly traded company and its cybersecurity protection is critical to your operations. The impact of a successful cyber-attack may have consequences that extend beyond your organization and impacts other market participants and retail investors, who may not be well informed of these risks and consequences.

What organization continues to prioritize cybersecurity in each of its five examination programs that focus on, among other things, proper configuration of network storage devices, information security governance generally, and policies and procedures related to retail trading information security.

Specific to investment advisers, what organization emphasizes cybersecurity practices at investment advisers with multiple branch offices, including those that have recently merged with other investment advisers, and continue to focus on, among other areas, governance and risk assessment, access rights and controls, data loss prevention, vendor management, training, and incident response?

Answers:

A. National Labor Relations Board
B. Occupational Safety and Health Act
C. Office of Compliance Inspections and Examinations
D. Department of Labor

CDPSE: FOCUSED PREPARATION

Question 89.

When a web server sends an HTML file to a client, it uses the hypertext transfer protocol (HTTP) to do so. The HTTP program layer asks this layer to set up the connection and send the file.

Although each packet in the transmission has the same source and destination IP address, packets may be sent along multiple routes.

Which communication protocol is this?

Answers:
A. HTTP
B. DNS
C. Network Layer
D. TCP

CDPSE: FOCUSED PREPARATION

Question 90.

Your organization operates a commercial website and online services that collect and maintain covered information from all of its consumers. Your organization is targeting a number of states and their residents. Which one of these states must you be compliant with their website privacy notification law?

Answers:

A. Minnesota
B. Colorado
C. Washington
D. Nevada

CDPSE: FOCUSED PREPARATION

Question 91.

Under the Fair and Accurate Credit Transaction Act (FACTA) organization's goals are all of these except:

Answers:

A. Notification
B. Prevention
C. Detection
D. Mitigation of identity theft

CDPSE: FOCUSED PREPARATION

Question 92.

Your organization, a private entity based in Illinois, captures biometric data for providing secure building access, tracking employee time and attendance, and authenticating users' identities for increased computer and mobile device login security.
Your organization has provided notice to the employees, obtained written consent and made certain disclosures.

What other requirement is needed by this organization?

Answers:

A. Develop a privacy notice
B. Develop the privacy program strategy
C. Develop a written HR policy
D. Develop a retention schedule

CDPSE: FOCUSED PREPARATION

Question 93.

The Fair and Accurate Credit Transactions Act (FACTA) adds provisions designed to promote data accuracy, fairness and privacy of information within the files of consumer reporting agencies. One requirement financial organizations must develop and implement are methods of detecting identity theft. What mandate is this called?

A.   Fair Credit Reporting Act (FCRA)
B.   Federal Trade Commission (FTC)
C.   Red Flags Rule
D.   Protective Order

CDPSE: FOCUSED PREPARATION

Question 94.

The Transactions and Code Sets standard within HIPAA was created to standardize the electronic exchange of patient-identifiable, health-related information.

It is based on electronic data interchange (EDI) standards, which allow the electronic exchange of information from computer to computer without human involvement.

How best would you integrate data within your business as the privacy solutions engineer?

Answers:

A. Conduct data inventory
B. Review asset management inventory
C. Conduct information data flow exercise
D. Outsource the solution

CDPSE: FOCUSED PREPARATION

Question 95.

This HIPAA Rule requires covered entities to notify affected individuals; HHS; and, in some cases, the media of a breach of unsecured PHI.

This rule also requires business associates of covered entities to notify the covered entity of breaches at or by the business associate.

Answers:

A. Privacy Rule
B. Security Rule
C. Enforcement Rule
D. Breach Notification Rule

CDPSE: FOCUSED PREPARATION

Question 96.

All 50 states, the District of Columbia (D.C), Puerto Rico and the U.S. Virgin Islands all have state data breach notification laws. Each state law varies, however, share the same basic elements. All of the following states include biometric data within their data breach laws, except:

Answers:

A. CT
B. MN
C. WI
D. NM

CDPSE: FOCUSED PREPARATION

Question 97.

Your organization is domiciled in Tennessee. Your organization encrypts and redacts the personal and business critical data. Your organization suffers a data breach. After you have contacted your data breach coach and deploy a forensic investigator, it is determined that your encryption key has not been compromised. Based on statutory requirements, how soon must you notify affected Tennessee residents of the data breach?

Answers:

A. 15 Days
B. 30 Days
C. 45 Days
D. 60 Days

CDPSE: FOCUSED PREPARATION

Question 98.

Consumer Online Privacy Rights Act (COPRA) and the United States Consumer Data Privacy Act (USCDPA) drafts are both addressing a key individual right.

The USCDPA contains no provision for this right. COPRA does have one (Section 301(c)), and it allows for all forms of relief within its draft. What right is being discussed?

Answers:

A. Class-action
B. Liability
C. Private Right of Action
D. Privacy Act

CDPSE: FOCUSED PREPARATION

Question 99.

Your organization encrypts and redacts the personal and business critical data it controls. Your organization suffers a data breach. After you have contacted your data breach coach and deploy a forensic investigator, it is determined that your encryption key has not been compromised. Based on Art. 33, who must you notify?

Answers:

A. Data Protection Authority
B. Supervisory Authority
C. Data Protection Officer
D. No one

CDPSE: FOCUSED PREPARATION

Question 100.

You, a citizen of a Member State, discovers and confirms that your information that is stored with a telecom organization (controller) is incorrect. Which GDPR article provides you the right to rectify that discrepancy?

Answers:

A. Art. 16
B. Art. 15
C. Art. 17
D. Art. 19

CDPSE: FOCUSED PREPARATION

Question 101.

The objective of this process is to assess an organization's privacy protection posture against any legislative/regulatory requirements or international best practices and to review compliance with the organization's own privacy-related policies.

The scope involves evaluating procedures undertaken by an organization throughout the typical information life-cycle phases: how information is created or received, distributed, used, maintained and eventually disposed of. As information and data have transformed from being scarce to superabundant, this process presents the status of risk associated with potential information misuse and recommends initiatives that can limit an organization's liability or reputational risk.

What is this process called?

Answers:

A. Privacy notice
B. Privacy impact assessment
C. Privacy audit process
D. Privacy risk assessment

CDPSE: FOCUSED PREPARATION

Question 102.

This is a standard that embodies many principles of interoperable and secure software for electronic health records. This work aims to understand to what extent the standard can be considered a solution for the requirements needed by GDPR.

What standard is this called?

Answers:

A. Electronic Health Record
B. Electronic Medical Record
C. OpenEHR
D. Privacy Standard

CDPSE: FOCUSED PREPARATION

Question 103.

The Coronavirus has impacted the globe both personally and professionally. Initial reports in March and April 2020 had five new cases a day being reported in areas, which was viewed as high. On November 4, 2020, over 100k cases were reported in one day within the U.S.
You are responsible for protecting the collection and reporting of this data within your privacy solutions engineer role.
What type of processing of personal data is this?

Answers:

A. Legitimate Interest
B. Public Interest
C. Consent
D. Contract

CDPSE: FOCUSED PREPARATION

Question 104.

The Directive on Patients' Rights in Cross-Border Healthcare provides a legal basis for establishing a network on e-health in order to address such practical issues, focusing in particular on cross-border aspects (such as summary records for cross-border care, identification and secure sharing of information), as well as the vital strategic issue of methods for using e-health to enable use of medical information for public health and research – potentially an answer to address the delays that currently plague health data.

The European Commission also finances a wide range of projects developing and piloting e-health technologies and applications, for example in support of the European Innovation Partnership on Active and Healthy Ageing. E-health is presented as a way to address the shortage of health professionals in the European Union, to ensure better care of ageing populations and chronic diseases putting pressure on health budgets, as well as to remedy unequal quality and access to healthcare services in Europe.
Which Article of the GDPR addresses personal health information?

Answers:

A. Art. 4
B. Art. 5
C. Art. 9
D. Art. 11

CDPSE: FOCUSED PREPARATION

Question 105.

An individual is applying for a new, open position listed on a job board website for your organization.

The application contains multiple 'yes or no' health-related questions. The application's Health History section states in large letters that "All questions must be answered before we can process your application."

The individual did not answer the questions based on their medical condition and disabilities due to had they have answered, they would have revealed those conditions and disabilities. Which Act is being violated here?

Answers:

A. Americans with Disabilities Act
B. EEOC
C. OSHA
D. National Labor Act

CDPSE: FOCUSED PREPARATION

Question 106.

The CFO and CHR of a manufacturing organization are looking to you, the privacy solutions engineer, to provide them with a performance measurement of the privacy protection program. Which of the following would you not utilize in creating that?

Answers:

A. Tracking
B. Identifying
C. Defining
D. Analyzing

CDPSE: FOCUSED PREPARATION

Question 107.

The FBI, HHS-OIG, and CMS have received complaints of scammers using the public's interest in COVID-19 vaccines to obtain personally identifiable information (PII) and money through various schemes.

The public should be aware of the following potential indicators of fraudulent activity:

- Advertisements or offers for early access to a vaccine upon payment of a deposit or fee
- Requests asking you to pay out of pocket to obtain the vaccine or to put your name on a COVID-19 vaccine waiting list
- Offers to undergo additional medical testing or procedures when obtaining a vaccine
- Marketers offering to sell and/or ship doses of a vaccine, domestically or internationally, in exchange for payment of a deposit or fee
- Unsolicited emails, telephone calls, or personal contact from someone claiming to be from a medical office, insurance company, or COVID-19 vaccine center requesting personal and/or medical information to determine recipients' eligibility to participate in clinical vaccine trials or obtain the vaccine
- Claims of FDA approval for a vaccine that cannot be verified
- Advertisements for vaccines through social media platforms, email, telephone calls, online, or from unsolicited/unknown sources
- Individuals contacting you in person, by phone, or by email to tell you the government or government officials require you to receive a COVID-19 vaccine

How can you as the privacy solutions engineer preempt both your organization's data and your patient's data from being compromised?

Answers:

A. Training and Awareness outreach programs
B. Privacy notice
C. Encryption
D. Role based access

CDPSE: FOCUSED PREPARATION

Question 108.

Your multinational organization is migrating their applications and processes to a cloud computing platform.
Accessibility, storage and management are key business drivers for this effort.

All of the following are challenges in cloud computing within GDPR except?

Answers:

A. Data retention
B. Data processing outside of the EEA
C. Data ownership
D. Vendor management

CDPSE: FOCUSED PREPARATION

Question 109.

Your organization has completed its data inventory and data retention policy has been compiled to overlay the data within the organization's possession.

As outlined in the GDPR, data destruction — designated as the elimination, erasure or clearing of digital content — is classified as a form of data processing. It also means any destruction procedures should follow the specific rules set forth by the regulation. Here are three steps that need to be followed:

Step 1: Step one is obviously to implement the appropriate controls allowing data owners full rights and permissions over their affected content. Companies must provide users with an option to delete all personal data — including sales or browsing histories. It absolutely must be a practical option that stems the flow of new content and eliminates the old as soon as possible.

Step 2: Businesses are also obligated to ensure old data or content is securely erased. Just deleting it via the operating system or server is not enough. In fact, reformatting old drives and magnetic media — including hard drives or audio tapes — is no guarantee, either. Deleted data can often be recovered provided the physical media is available.

Step 3: It's important to properly dispose of?

Answers:

A. Hardware
B. Software
C. Records
D. Cloud storage

CDPSE: FOCUSED PREPARATION

Question 110.

This technology is a decentralized data structure where the data is distributed across all computers or nodes within a network and every node in the network stores a copy of the ledger.
There is no central administration of the data and the data are agreed upon by consensus by all nodes in the network.
This technology leverages decentralized peer-to-peer computing, cryptography and related technology to verify and propagate a chain of transaction records across a consortium, alliance, partnership, or coalition.

What technology is this?

Answers:

A. Blockchain technology
B. Distributed ledger technology
C. Server technology
D. Internet of Things technology

CDPSE: FOCUSED PREPARATION

Question 111.

The National Institute of Standards and Technology (NIST) defines this as "tamper evident and tamper resistant digital ledgers implemented in a distributed fashion (i.e., without a central repository) and usually without a central authority ([e.g.,] a bank, company, or government).

At [its] basic level, it enable[s] a community of users to record transactions in a shared ledger within that community, such that under normal operation of the network no transaction can be changed once published."

What is this?

Answers:

A. Blockchain
B. DLT
C. Cryptography
D. Cryptocurrency

CDPSE: FOCUSED PREPARATION

Question 112.

IT systems form the backbone of every organization, including all financial firms.

Client data continually passes through multiple IT applications and these firms need to understand all data flows across their various systems. The increased trend towards outsourcing development and support functions means that personal client data is often accessed by external vendors, thus significantly increasing the data's net exposure.

Under GDPR, vendors cannot disassociate themselves from obligations towards data access. Similarly, non-EU organizations working in collaboration with EU banks or serving EU citizens need to ensure vigilance while sharing data across borders. GDPR in effect imposes end-to-end accountability to ensure client data stays well protected by enforcing not only the bank, but all its support functions to embrace compliance.

What management program would this best fall under within your governance program?

Answers:

A. Vendor management
B. Risk management
C. Supply chain contingency plan
D. Governance program

CDPSE: FOCUSED PREPARATION

Question 113.

This process ensures that the organization understands, inventories, maps, and controls its data, as it is created and modified through business processes throughout the data lifecycle, from creation or acquisition to retirement.

What is this called?

Answers:

A. Storage
B. Data lifecycle management
C. Creation
D. Destruction

CDPSE: FOCUSED PREPARATION

Question 114.

All of the following are phases within this management process.
Create, Store, Use, Share, Archive, and Destroy.

What process is this?

Answers:

A. Data Retention Management
B. Records Management
C. Policy Management
D. Data Lifecycle Management

CDPSE: FOCUSED PREPARATION

Question 115.

This principle in healthcare allows for the accessible and actionable exchange of clinical information — including the insights extracted from EHR, medical imaging systems, and other sources — among providers to streamline patient care.

What is this called?

Answers:

A. Vendor Management
B. Business Associate
C. Interconnectivity
D. ACE

CDPSE: FOCUSED PREPARATION

Question 116.

This trust model makes sure that multinational organizations can monitor all attempts at exploiting the vulnerabilities inherent in these web applications and connections.

It can help these organizations provision access in a more effective manner by focusing on data, workloads and identity.

What trust model is this?

Answers:

A. Direct trust
B. Transitive trust
C. Zero trust
D. Assumptive trust

CDPSE: FOCUSED PREPARATION

Question 117.

This technology comprises interconnected medical devices and applications that collect data, which is then provided to healthcare IT systems through online computer networks.

For example, smart beds, wearable medical devices, infusion pumps, and embedded devices are all new technologies in this category. These devices present major benefits to providers and patients such as improved drug management, process automation, and enhanced data analytics across multiple domains, improved patient outcomes, and remote patient monitoring.

What is this technology?

Answers:

A. Internet of Things
B. Internet of Medical Things
C. Internet
D. Zero Trust

CDPSE: FOCUSED PREPARATION

Question 118.

This control is about enforcing rules to ensure that only authorized users get access to resources in a system. In healthcare systems this means protecting patient privacy.

This control may be in the physical, administrative, or technical control families.

What control is this?

Answer:

A. HR controls
B. Configuration Management controls
C. Awareness and Training controls
D. Access controls

CDPSE: FOCUSED PREPARATION

Question 119.

This is an authentication system that requires more than one distinct authentication factor for successful authentication. This can be performed using an authenticator or by a combination of authenticators that provide different factors. The three authentication factors are something you know, something you have, and something you are.

What type of authentication is this?

Answers:

A. Single-factor authentication
B. Dual authorization
C. Multi-factor authentication
D. Authentication

CDPSE: FOCUSED PREPARATION

Question 120.

Your medical staff has access to all EMRs. Each staff member is trained frequently on proper handling, access, and protecting of sensitive data. If one of your medical practitioners is unable to access an EMR, and is authorized to access it, which basic security principle has been applied?

Answers:

A. Role-Based Access
B. Segregation of duties
C. Least privilege
D. Need-to-know access

CDPSE: FOCUSED PREPARATION

Question 121.

A fundamental part of securing your organization's information is knowing what data you have and who can access it. It's the process of identifying and assigning predetermined levels of sensitivity to different types of information.

This not only means understanding what types of data you own, but what you're doing with it. For example, your organization is a financial institution which holds a person's mortgage application, which contains a wealth of Non-Public Personal Information (NPPI) like income level, current home address, their previous home address, other loan information, and more.

This information needs to be protected. However, the level of protection that is applied depends on the?

A. Privacy Policy
B. Data classification it is assigned
C. Technical controls applied
D. Role-Based Access applied

CDPSE: FOCUSED PREPARATION

Question 122.

Your medical staff has access to all EMRs. Each staff member is trained frequently on proper handling, access, and protecting of sensitive data. If one of your medical practitioners accesses an EMR in which they did not and will not provide care to, which basic security principle has been violated?

Answers:

A. Role-Based Access
B. Segregation of duties
C. Least privilege
D. Need-to-know access

CDPSE: FOCUSED PREPARATION

Question 123.

Your organization processes and collects over 1,000,000 credit card transactions annually.

You have conducted an assessment on your PCI-DSS compliance. Prior to finalizing your report of compliance (ROC), you suffer a data breach and identify that your organization did not report nor respond to the breach in an adequate time frame.

What control might not be implemented within your program?

Answers:

A. Phishing training
B. Special handling training
C. Information security
D. Incident response plan

CDPSE: FOCUSED PREPARATION

Question 124.

With COVID-19 still upon us and a number of organizations continuing to work-from-home, remote access for both internal and external sources has increased over the past year.

Remote Desktop Protocol (RDP), the Microsoft Windows component that makes it easy for your employees to connect to work or home computers while they are away, is used by millions.

While RDP operates on an encrypted channel on servers, there is a vulnerability in the encryption method in earlier versions of RDP, making it a preferred gateway by hackers.

For companies that not only want to meet compliance standards but exceed them, RDP security is a challenge. While RDP is built into Microsoft operating systems, it can also be installed on Apple, Linux, and Android operating systems.

Without properly securing it, your RDP can become the gateway where a malware infection or targeted ransomware is deployed, resulting in critical service disruption.

What is the first step in defending against RDP security risks?

Answers:

A. Block TCP port 3389
B. Enabling Network Level Authentication (NLA)
C. Creating a policy to handle endpoints ensuring the port isn't accessible to the internet
D. Limit RDP remote users

CDPSE: FOCUSED PREPARATION

Question 125.

It is Monday morning, and you are starting a new role as the privacy solutions engineer.

You log into your corporate email account and find an email from HR. As you read through the email, you see that you are required to complete specific privacy training. What type of control is this?

A. Special Handling
B. Data Classification
C. Technical
D. Role-Based Access

CDPSE: FOCUSED PREPARATION

Question 126.

This is a crucial part of developing any web or mobile application. It is the combination of programming languages and software underneath a development project.

This, also called a technology infrastructure, or a data ecosystem, is a list of all the technology services used to build and run one single application.

A social media platform may be composed of a combination of coding frameworks and languages including JavaScript, HTML, CSS, PHP, and ReactJS.

What is this called?

Answers:

A. PaaS
B. Technology stack
C. CaaS
D. Infrastructure inventory

CDPSE: FOCUSED PREPARATION

Question 127.

Your organization provides time-sensitive and business sensitive documents and information to your customer, allowing their users to interact with the application in a web browser to upload and interact with both your files and theirs, but all of the data processing and storage happens remotely on the cloud.

What is the name of this type of service?

A. Content management system
B. Cloud-as-a-Services
C. Platform-as-a-Service
D. Software-as-a-Service

CDPSE: FOCUSED PREPARATION

Question 128.

A requirement consisting of locking down all systems within an organization that is capable of obtaining internal access to resources forces privacy solution professionals to look at every possible access route that may be exploited in launching an attack falls into this type of security control

These systems are the most vulnerable components of your computing environment. Implementing these systems and devices with anti-virus software, multi-factor authentication, and automated application updates are simple protections that supplement your organization in securing both yours and any customers or client's data.

What type of security is this?

Answers:

A. Cloud security
B. Remote access
C. Endpoint protection
D. System security

CDPSE: FOCUSED PREPARATION

Question 129.

What type of data is not considered to be personal data by the GDPR, as detailed in Article 4(1), and its collection and processing is governed by the GDPR. Article 3(2) states that, "This Regulation applies to the processing of personal data of data subjects who are in the Union."

Answers:

A. Geolocation
B. Online identifier
C. Economic
D. Historic

CDPSE: FOCUSED PREPARATION

Question 130.

In 1996, the Department of Health and Human Services within the United States of America, signed into law the Healthcare Insurance Portability and Accountability Act (HIPAA). HIPAA was created to "improve the portability and accountability of health insurance coverage" for employees between jobs.
Within GDPR, Art. 20 empowers the data subject to have the right receive the personal data concerning him or her, which he or she has provided to a controller, in a structured, commonly used and machine-readable format and have the right to transmit those data to another controller without hindrance from the controller to which the personal data have been provided. This right is what?

A. Access
B. Rectification
C. Data portability
D. Automated decision making

CDPSE: FOCUSED PREPARATION

Question 131.

As your organization decides on what data to collect, it must identify valid business purposes, known as a lawful basis, for collecting and using personal data. Art. 5(1) of the GDPR outlines six data protection principles. Which is the first?

Answers:

A. Purpose limitation
B. Data minimization
C. Accuracy
D. Fairness

CDPSE: FOCUSED PREPARATION

Question 132.

GDPR non-compliant fines are based on the specific articles of the Regulation that the organization has breached. Infringements of the organization's obligations, including data security breaches, will be subject to the lower level, whereas infringements of an individual's privacy rights will be subject to the higher level. Data controllers and processors face administrative fines of the higher of €10 million or 2% of annual global turnover for infringements of articles:
8 (conditions for children's consent),
11 (processing that doesn't require identification),
25-39 (general obligations of processors and controllers),
42 (certification), and
43 (certification bodies)

The higher of €20 million or 4% of annual global turnover for infringements of articles:
5 (data processing principles),
6 (lawful bases for processing),
7 (conditions for consent),
9 (processing of special categories of data),
12-22 (data subjects' rights), and
44-49 (data transfers to third countries).

In 2019, British Airways was fined what amount for a 2018 data breach over data security failings which enabled unauthorized access to be obtained to personal and payment card information relating to more than 500,000 of its customers.

Answers:

A. €10 million
B. €20 million
C. €183 million
D. €30 million

CDPSE: FOCUSED PREPARATION

Question 133.

Your organization has implemented a new encryption solution for your stored data.
If your encryption keys become compromised, an unauthorized user may use those keys to:

- Create phishing websites impersonating your original website;
- Pass through your corporate networks by impersonating you or your employees;
- Sign applications or documents in your name;
- Extract/tamper with the data stored on the server; and/or
- Read your encrypted emails and do any number of nefarious things.

If a cyber perpetrator has your keys, they can do any — or all — of that to their benefit and your detriment. They can use your keys to make money by asking for ransom, sell your data to your competitors, go share them on public platforms and ruin your reputation.

No organization wants any of that to happen. That's why encryption key management should be one of your top priorities as far as data security and privacy is concerned.

What NIST standard would you consult for assistance in developing a key management program?

Answers:

A. NIST Special Publication 800-57 part 1, rev. 5
B. NIST Special Publication 800-63 rev. 4
C. NIST Special Publication 800-171 rev. 2
D. NIST Special Publication 800-39

CDPSE: FOCUSED PREPARATION

Question 134.

You are the privacy solutions engineer within your organization. Your organization processes personal data wholly or partly by automated means and the processing other than by automated means of personal data which do form part of a filing system or are intended to form a filing system applies to which GDPR article?

Answers:

A. Art. 2
B. Art. 3
C. Art. 1
D. Art. 4

CDPSE: FOCUSED PREPARATION

Question 135.

You are the privacy solutions engineer within your organization. Your organization processes personal data of data subjects who are in the Union by a controller or processor not established in the Union, where the processing activities are related to the offering of goods or services. Which GDPR article applies?

Answers:

A. Art. 2
B. Art. 3
C. Art. 1
D. Art. 4

CDPSE: FOCUSED PREPARATION

Question 136.

Your organization completed the data inventory exercise. What term is explicitly highlighted in Article 6(4)(e) as an "appropriate safeguard" that can be used by data controllers "in order to ascertain whether processing for another purpose is compatible with the purpose for which the personal data are initially collected?

Answers:

A. Data minimization
B. Anonymize
C. Pseudonymization
D. Data encryption

Question 137.

Which data protection principle entails that personal data must be kept in a form that makes it possible to identify data subjects for no longer than is necessary for the purposes of the processing. Keeping these data for longer periods is allowed when the processing of the data will aim at achieving purposes in the public interest, scientific or historical research purposes or statistical purposes. Nevertheless, also in these cases rights and freedoms of data subjects must be safeguarded.

Answers:

A. Purpose limitation
B. Storage
C. Integrity and Confidentiality
D. Accuracy

CDPSE: FOCUSED PREPARATION

Question 138.

What does a trusted platform module utilized to secure both a key and software on a system provide your organization?

Answers:

A. Speeds up the encryption process utilizing the system bus
B. Guarantees confidentiality of the system data
C. Secures data until other conditions are met
D. Ensures the encryption key will never be utilized outside of its system

CDPSE: FOCUSED PREPARATION

Question 139.

While in the maintenance stage within the System Development Life Cycle (SDLC), a vulnerability is discovered.

What actions must be taken?

Answers:

A. Report the vulnerability
B. Make changes following the guidelines
C. Stop the application development and mitigate the vulnerability
D. Monitor the application and review code

CDPSE: FOCUSED PREPARATION

Question 140.

Your organization is working on implementing and protecting the contact tracing applications that it utilizes. You have built application programming interfaces (API) and other applications to support this project.

A few questions you have been asking and documenting answers provided are to what data is being collected and who is this data being shared with.

You compile your final report and highlight a few of the risks identified that your organization must address.

Which of the following are not risks associated with tracking technologies?

Answers:

A. Geo-location tracking
B. Beacon-based tracking
C. Online behavioral tracking
D. Financial expense tracking

CDPSE: FOCUSED PREPARATION

Question 141.

You, the privacy solutions engineer for your organization, is designing processes and procedures for protecting applications from being reverse engineered back to its source code and from bad actors inspecting internal values, monitoring or tampering with the application.

What type of security controls are you executing?

Answers:

A. Software hardening
B. Secure Development Lifecycle
C. Application hardening
D. System hardening

CDPSE: FOCUSED PREPARATION

Question 142.

In order for data classification to work, the data should meet some criteria that enable a decision to be made about what classification applies.
The presence of one of the following two capabilities should be applied.
-An automated system that can analyze the data and apply rules to make that decision
-An interface for users to create, verify or override a classification.
-Discovery in a variety of data storage environments is a key capability for automated systems.
-The provision of a recording of that classification that allows other systems and processes to leverage that decision.
-The inclusion of a log, dashboard or other method to allow data and security administrators to understand the data estate for a variety of reasons.

Where does the data classification program add value to?

Answers:

A. Information Asset Identification
B. Asset Valuation
C. Risk Assessment
D. Risk Management

CDPSE: FOCUSED PREPARATION

Question 143.

You are consulting with your information security team on new lifecycle processes.
You are promoting the incorporation of data protection via their technology designs and infrastructure implementations.
You remember that you can have security without privacy, however, you cannot have privacy without security.
What design model is this referencing?

Answers:

A. Privacy by Default
B. Privacy by Design
C. Integrity and Confidentiality
D. Privacy Program

CDPSE: FOCUSED PREPARATION

Question 144.

You are the new risk management professional in an international organization.

You have applied your asset valuation exercise to your most critical assets across the globe and are in the process of gathering new global threats and vulnerabilities applicable to your organization.

When reviewing the current risk management framework, you determine that it may not be as robust and focused on international risk management.

Which of the following frameworks might better suit your organization?

Answers:

A. ISO 27005:2018
B. ISO 31000:2018
C. ISO 27799:2016
D. NIST SP 800-53Rev4

CDPSE: FOCUSED PREPARATION

Question 145.

Asymmetric algorithms are utilized for which of the following when using SSL/TLS for implementing network security?

Answers:

A. Encryption
B. Session encryption
C. Peer encryption
D. Payload data encryption

CDPSE: FOCUSED PREPARATION

Question 146.

Which of the following risk management lifecycle processes is where the implemented control is verified for the effectiveness based on the stated control objectives?

Answers:

A. Plan
B. Do
C. Check
D. Act

CDPSE: FOCUSED PREPARATION

Question 147.

On July 16, 2020, the CJEU invalidated the E.U.-U.S. Privacy Shield, one of the methods for transfers of personal data into the U.S. The court found that under U.S. surveillance laws, the U.S. government has access to personal data that does not provide Europeans with privacy protections equivalent to those in the E.U.
Which answer below is most associated with this ruling?

Answers:

A. Schrems
B. Snowden
C. GDRP
D. Privacy Protection

CDPSE: FOCUSED PREPARATION

Question 148.

Your organization is developing its data storage strategy and incorporating security, privacy, costs, analytics and more.

All of the following are critical risks to the data except?

Answers:

A. Incompetent analytics
B. Data destruction
C. Cost management
D. Data gravity

CDPSE: FOCUSED PREPARATION

Question 149.

As your organization researches best practices for data destruction, it reviews all of the data and medium's its data resides on.

What is the best practice?

Answers:

A. Physical destruction
B. Degaussing
C. Overwriting
D. Deleting

CDPSE: FOCUSED PREPARATION

Question 150.

De-identification and anonymization are strategies that are used to remove patient identifiers in electronic health record (EHR) data. The use of these strategies in multicenter research studies is paramount in importance, given the need to share EHR data across multiple environments and institutions while safeguarding patient privacy.

What method is best for de-identification of data?

Answers:

A. Encryption
B. Pseudonymization
C. Removal of specified individual identifiers
D. Anonymization

CDPSE: FOCUSED PREPARATION

Answer Key:

1. D	41. C	81. C
2. D	42. A	82. A
3. D	43. A	83. D
4. C	44. B	84. B
5. A	45. C	85. A
6. B	46. B	86. C
7. D	47. B	87. B
8. B	48. B	88. C
9. A	49. C	89. D
10. C	50. C	90. D
11. D	51. D	91. A
12. D	52. C	92. D
13. B	53. A	93. C
14. D	54. D	94. B
15. C	55. A	95. D
16. C	56. B	96. B
17. B	57. C	97. C
18. C	58. A	98. C
19. D	59. B	99. D
20. D	60. A	100. A
21. D	61. D	101. C
22. D	62. D	102. C
23. B	63. D	103. B
24. A	64. B	104. C
25. D	65. D	105. A
26. C	66. D	106. B
27. C	67. D	107. A
28. B	68. B	108. D
29. D	69. C	109. A
30. B	70. B	110. B
31. C	71. D	111. A
32. D	72. C	112. A
33. C	73. D	113. B
34. A	74. D	114. D
35. D	75. A	115. C
36. A	76. D	116. C
37. C	77. C	117. B
38. B	78. D	118. D
39. A	79. B	119. C
40. C	80. C	120. C

CDPSE: FOCUSED PREPARATION

Answer Key (cont):

121. B
122. D
123. D
124. C
125. D
126. B
127. A
128. C
129. D
130. C
131. D
132. C
133. A
134. A
135. B
136. C
137. B
138. A
139. B
140. D
141. C
142. B
143. B
144. B
145. D
146. C
147. A
148. D
149. A
150. C

CDPSE: FOCUSED PREPARATION

Question with Answers:

Question 1.

Technologies that enable and enhance and preserve privacy and security of data throughout its entire lifecycle while protecting information privacy by eliminating or minimizing personal data is called?

<u>Technologies</u> that enable and enhance and <u>preserve privacy</u> and security of <u>data</u> throughout its entire <u>lifecycle</u> while protecting <u>information privacy</u> by <u>eliminating</u> or <u>minimizing personal data</u> is called?

Key words: Technologies; preserve privacy; data; lifecycle; information privacy; eliminating; minimizing personal data

Questions to ask yourself – What technologies preserve privacy/data?; What is information lifecycle (term)? What does minimizing personal data mean?

Answers:

A. Confidentiality
B. Data Protection
C. Information Security
D. Privacy Enabling Technologies

The correct answer is D. Privacy Enabling Technologies (PET) are tools that simply enable privacy. PETs fall under the paradigm of Privacy by Design (PbD) and within the privacy engineering discipline.

CDPSE: FOCUSED PREPARATION

Question 2.

The privacy framework for transpacific exchanges of personal data between Asia-Pacific and the United States is called?

The <u>privacy framework</u> for <u>transpacific exchanges</u> of <u>personal data</u> between <u>Asia-Pacific</u> and the <u>United States</u> is called?

Key words: privacy framework; transpacific exchanges; personal data; Asia-Pacific; United States

Questions to ask yourself – What is a privacy framework? What framework applies to transpacific personal data exchanges? What framework applies to Asia Pacific and the United States?

Answers:

A. General Data Protection Regulation
B. Privacy Shield
C. Organization for Economic Co-operation and Development Transborder Flow
D. Asia-Pacific Economic Cooperation (APEC) Privacy Framework

The correct answer is D.

Answers A and C are geared towards information security risk management and the question does not ask for information security risk management information.

CDPSE: FOCUSED PREPARATION

Question 3.

The right of a human individual to control the distribution of information about him or herself is called?

The <u>right</u> of a human individual to <u>control</u> the <u>distribution</u> of <u>information</u> about him or herself is called?

Key words: right; control; distribution; information

Questions to ask yourself – What is a right of a human?; What control do I have of my information? Who do I want to have my information?

Answers:

A. Confidentiality
B. Data Protection
C. Information Security
D. Privacy

The correct answer is D. Privacy is not written in our U.S. Constitution. Privacy is the right to be left alone, protection of personal data and numerous other similar definitions.

Answer A is preserving authorized restrictions on information access and disclosure, including means for protecting personal privacy and proprietary information.

Answer B refers to the processes and controls to protect personal information.

Answer C is a set of practices to keep data secure from unauthorized access or alterations.

All of these are collectively protecting – actions in protecting your privacy.

CDPSE: FOCUSED PREPARATION

Question 4.

On July 16, 2020, the European Union Court of Justice (CJEU) invalidated the EU-US Privacy Shield in its decision in Facebook Ireland v. Schrems (Schrems II). The court determined that the Privacy Shield transfer mechanism does not comply with the level of protection required under EU law.
The decision reinforces the European Union's commitment to protecting what?

On July 16, 2020, the <u>European Union Court of Justice (CJEU)</u> <u>invalidated</u> the <u>EU-US Privacy Shield</u> in its decision in Facebook Ireland v. Schrems (Schrems II). The court determined that the Privacy Shield <u>transfer mechanism</u> does <u>not comply</u> with the <u>level of protection</u> required under EU law.
The decision reinforces the European Union's commitment to protecting what?

Key words: European Union Court of Justice; invalidated; EU-US Privacy Shield; transfer mechanism; not comply; level of protection

Questions to ask yourself – What is being transferred? What did the EU-US Privacy Shield provide organizations?

Answers:

A. Regulations
B. Security
C. Privacy
D. Citizens

The correct answer is C. The full answer would be the privacy of member's data. Answer D is incorrect. Had the question been presented differently around protecting an individual and not discussing Privacy Shield and levels of protection, perhaps then, answer D might have been a possible answer.
You will see questions that infer information that you must draw from and piece together for the correct answer on your actual exam. If you knew what Privacy Shield was and why it was created, you would then understand that protecting members' data privacy would be key.

CDPSE: FOCUSED PREPARATION

Question 5.

Defense in Depth (DiD) models allow your organization to apply several layers (depth) of controls across its perimeter to protect the organization's assets.
The DiD model promotes the possible breach of multiple, exterior depth controls before being detected and responded to.
One key access control that, if implemented, will protect your core assets is the?

Answers:

E. Principle of Least Privilege (PoLP)
F. Trust Model
G. Security Guard
H. Training and Awareness

The correct answer is A. PoLP is a policy in which end users are given only the amount of access they need to carry out their jobs — nothing more and nothing less.

Answer B is distracting, incorrect answer.

Answer C is incorrect.

Answer D is a distracting, incorrect answer.

CDPSE: FOCUSED PREPARATION

Question 6.

You are the privacy solutions engineer professional within your multinational organization and are reviewing proposed new technologies being requested for implementation within your facilities. You conduct an analysis of how information is handled, ensuring that the handling is in compliance with legal, regulatory and policy requirements regarding privacy that your organization is accountable to and for.

What is this analysis?

Answers:

E. Privacy Notice
F. Privacy Impact Assessment
G. Data Protection Impact Assessment
H. Privacy Audit

The correct answer is B. The PIA is an assessment of an organization's compliance with its privacy policies and procedures, applicable laws, regulations, service-level agreements, standards adopted by the entity and other contracts. A PIA also discloses what PII is being collected, why it is being collected, what the intended uses of the PII are, whom the PII will be shared with, and an analysis of the information life cycle.

Answer C is, in accordance with Article 35, Data protection impact assessment, of the GDPR: Where a type of processing in particular using new technologies, and taking into account the nature, scope, context and purposes of the processing, is likely to result in a high risk to the rights and freedoms of natural persons, the controller shall, prior to the processing, carry out an assessment of the impact of the envisaged processing operations on the protection of personal data.
A data protection impact assessment shall in particular be required in the case of processing on a large scale of special categories of data referred to in Article 9(1).

Answer A is a statement made to a data subject that describes how an organization collects, uses, retains and discloses personal information.

Answer B is an assessment of an organization's compliance with its privacy policies and procedures, applicable laws, regulations, service-level agreements, standards adopted by the entity and other contracts.

Answer C, also known as a privacy compliance audit, is an assessment tool that looks at an organization's privacy protection policies and procedures, specifically in light of current relevant laws or regulatory requirements.

CDPSE: FOCUSED PREPARATION

Question 7.

Your organization recently conducted its semi-annually risk assessment. Throughout the assessment, multiple findings were identified, verified with different responses.

The reason your organization conducts a semi-annual assessment is due to the following that constitute risk assessment factors: Number of breaches; number of outages; unauthorized access; lost assets; software viruses; investigations.

Multiple risks identified were dodged. Numerous risks were agreed on. Others were alleviated and others are protected by a cyber insurance program.

What is the last action called from the risk response strategies?

Answers:

E. Avoidance
F. Acceptance
G. Mitigation
H. Transfer

The correct answer is D. Transfer of risks generally includes transferring those unacceptable risks to an insurance policy.

Answer A is another term for dodged.
Answer B is another term for acceptance.
Answer C is another term for alleviated.

CDPSE: FOCUSED PREPARATION

Question 8.

The National Institute of Standards and Technology (NIST) developed a six-step process for the Risk Management Framework (RMF), and one of those 6 steps helps management to review business processes 24/7 to see if the performance, effectiveness and efficiency are achieving the anticipated targets, or if there is something deviating from the intended targets.

Your multinational organization utilizes the RMF along with a formal process of defining its IT systems, categorizing each of these systems by the level of risk, application of the controls, continuous monitoring of the applied controls, and the assessment of the effectiveness of these controls against security threats.

What is this process named?

Answers:

E. Continuous Control Monitoring
F. Continuous Monitoring
G. Program Management
H. Risk Assessment Process

The correct answer is B. Technology is an integral part of all business processes, but the ever-increasing threats to cybersecurity have given rise to the importance of a foolproof Continuous Monitoring Program.

Bad actors and cyber threats continue to happen, and changes occur in the blink of an eye.

Continuous monitoring is important because the process is skeptical about potential threats. A good continuous monitoring program is the one that is flexible and features highly reliable, relevant and effective controls to deal with the potential threats.

CDPSE: FOCUSED PREPARATION

Question 9.

You are the privacy solutions engineer of your multinational organization and have conducted your data inventory exercise. You are now in the process of implementing a roadmap that provides the structure or checklists (documented privacy procedures and processes) to guide the privacy solutions engineer through privacy management and prompts them for the details to determine all privacy-relevant decisions for the organization.

This process is a certifiable framework that provides organizations with a comprehensive, flexible, and an efficient approach to regulatory compliance and risk management and ties into processes and programs. What is this process called?

Answers:

E. Privacy Program Framework (PPM)
F. HITRUST Cybersecurity Framework (CSF)
G. NIST Cybersecurity Framework (CSF)
H. NIST Privacy Framework (PF)

The correct answer is A. The International Association of Privacy Professionals (IAPP) is a nonprofit, non-advocacy membership association founded in 2000 and is responsible for developing and launching and leading global credentialing programs in information privacy.

IAPP's definition of a PPM is, 'An implementation roadmap that provides the structure or checklists (documented privacy procedures and processes) to guide the privacy professional through privacy management and prompts them for the details to determine all privacy-relevant decisions for the organization.'

Answer B provides the structure, transparency, guidance, and cross-references to authoritative sources organizations globally need to be certain of their data protection compliance. The initial development of the HITRUST CSF leveraged nationally and internationally accepted security and privacy-related regulations, standards, and frameworks–including ISO, NIST, PCI, HIPAA, and COBIT–to ensure a comprehensive set of security and privacy controls, and continually incorporates additional authoritative sources. The HITRUST CSF standardizes these requirements, providing clarity and consistency, and reducing the burden of compliance.

Answer C is a set of guidelines for private sector companies to follow to be better prepared in identifying, detecting, and responding to cyber-attacks. It also includes guidelines on how to prevent and recover from an attack.

Answer D is a voluntary tool developed in collaboration with stakeholders intended to help organizations identify and manage privacy risk to build innovative products and services while protecting individuals' privacy.

CDPSE: FOCUSED PREPARATION

Question 10.

Your pharmaceutical organization has continued to grow and mature its overall privacy and security posture.
You are reviewing all current privacy and security policies for any gaps based on your regulatory mapping and data flow paths that have been documented.
The security team is overlaying their security controls along the data flow path, both internally and externally.
You are continuing to review all contracts where sensitive information is being shared or disclosed and updating requirements for both privacy and security measures to be applied.
As you review all controls in place and strategically planned to be implemented, your privacy and security teams have controls that support identifying, protecting, detecting, responding, and recovering controls across your entire organization.
Which framework have you implemented?

Answers:

E. Privacy Program Framework (PPM)
F. HITRUST Cybersecurity Framework (CSF)
G. NIST Cybersecurity Framework (CSF)
H. NIST Privacy Framework (PF)

The correct answer is C. The NIST CSF is a set of guidelines for private sector companies to follow to be better prepared in identifying, detecting, and responding to cyber-attacks. It also includes guidelines on how to prevent and recover from an attack.

Answer A is a roadmap that provides the structure or checklists (documented privacy procedures and processes) to guide the privacy solutions engineer through privacy management and prompts them for the details to determine all privacy-relevant decisions for the organization.'

Answer B provides the structure, transparency, guidance, and cross-references to authoritative sources organizations globally need to be certain of their data protection compliance. The initial development of the HITRUST CSF leveraged nationally and internationally accepted security and privacy-related regulations, standards, and frameworks—including ISO, NIST, PCI, HIPAA, and COBIT—to ensure a comprehensive set of security and privacy controls, and continually incorporates additional authoritative sources. The HITRUST CSF standardizes these requirements, providing clarity and consistency, and reducing the burden of compliance.

Answer D is a voluntary tool developed in collaboration with stakeholders intended to help organizations identify and manage privacy risk to build innovative products and services while protecting individuals' privacy.

CDPSE: FOCUSED PREPARATION

Question 11.

Your multinational healthcare organization is preparing to share ePHI with multiple processors. You are reviewing Article 4(5) of the GDPR for guidance.
What is the processing of protected personal data in such a manner that the personal data can no longer be attributed to a specific data subject without the use of additional information, provided that such additional information is kept separately and is subject to technical and organizational measures to ensure that the personal data are not attributed to an identified or identifiable natural person?

Answers:

E. Cleansed
F. Disposed
G. Encrypted
H. Pseudonymized

The correct answer is D. In other words, pseudonymization is the process of replacing identifying or sensitive data with a pseudonym. This is synonymous with tokenization, which replaces sensitive data with a non-sensitive placeholder called a token, a technology utilized for years by the Payment Card Industry to protect payment card information (PCI).

CDPSE: FOCUSED PREPARATION

Question 12.

Your multinational healthcare organization is conducting cross-border transfers of electronic protected health information from multiple Asia-Pacific regions to other regions.

Your cross-border transfer program framework consists of all of the following within the Asia-Pacific (APEC) Privacy Framework objectives, except the following:

Answers:

E. To prevent harm
F. To limit collection
G. To provide choice
H. To encrypt data

The correct answer is D. The following are the primary objectives of the APEC Privacy Framework:

Prevent Harm; Provide Notice; Limit Collection; Control Use; Provide Choice; Ensure Integrity; Use Appropriate Security Safeguards; Allow Access and Correction; and Be Accountable.

Although encryption *may be* an appropriate security safeguard, it is not one of the listed objectives and there may be other, similar types of security safeguards that will protect the data appropriately.

CDPSE: FOCUSED PREPARATION

Question 13.

General Data Protection Law (LGPD) is Brazil's first comprehensive data protection law and is designed to enhance the privacy and protection of personal data of individuals in Brazil. The LGPD heavily resembles the EU General Data Protection Regulation (GDPR).

On September 17, 2020, the Brazilian president approved the bill, resulting in the LGPD taking effect on September 18, 2020.

At the end of October 2020, India announced that they are currently working towards a privacy regulation, similar, yet possibly more stringent than GDPR? What will this new law be named?

Answers:

A. General Data Protection Regulation (GDPR)
B. Personal Data Protection Act (PDPA)
C. Privacy Data Protection Act (PrDPA)
D. Personal Privacy Rights Act (PPRA)

The correct answer is B. The proposed naming convention of the Indian privacy regulation is Personal Data Protection Act (PDPA).
Answer C and D are distractors.

CDPSE: FOCUSED PREPARATION

Question 14.

You are the privacy solutions engineer within your U.S. domiciled healthcare organization. You have been reviewing the Department of Health and Human Services (HHS) website for recent fines and penalties levied against other organizations to determine if your organization has similar risks.

You have reviewed multiple complaints that have been submitted to your organization based on different components and protocols.

You know that if the OCR accepts a complaint for investigation, the OCR will notify the person who filed the complaint and the covered entity named in it. Then the complainant and the covered entity are asked to present information about the incident or problem described in the complaint.

The OCR may request specific information from each to get an understanding of the facts. Covered entities are required by law to cooperate with complaint investigations.

The OCR reviews the information, or evidence, that it gathers in each case. In some cases, it may determine that the covered entity did not violate the requirements of the Privacy or Security Rule. If the evidence indicates that the covered entity was not in compliance, OCR will attempt to resolve the case with the covered entity by obtaining each of these except:

Answers:

E. Voluntary compliance
F. Corrective action
G. Resolution agreement
H. Consent decree

The correct answer is D. The other three answers are what the OCR will attempt to obtain. A consent decree, enforced by the U.S. Federal Trade Commission (FTC), is a judgment entered by consent of the parties. Typically, the defendant agrees to stop alleged illegal activity and pay a fine, without admitting guilt or wrongdoing. This legal document is approved by a judge and formalizes an agreement reached between a U.S. federal or state agency and an adverse party.

CDPSE: FOCUSED PREPARATION

Question 15.

You are the privacy solutions engineer for a small retail organization that is conducting a self-regulatory self-assessment questionnaire (SAQ). Which one of these would this report best support?

Answers:

A. GDPR
B. EU Directive on Electronic Commerce
C. PCI DSS
D. U.S. HIPAA

The correct answer is C. Payment Card Industry Data Security Standard (PCI-DSS) is not a law or regulation. It's a standard that the four major credit card companies have adopted that tells merchants, essentially, if you want to collect payments from customers using credit and debit cards you must adhere to the PCI standard.

The European Union Agency for Cybersecurity, ENISA, is the Union's agency dedicated to achieving a high common level of cybersecurity across Europe. Established in 2004 and strengthened by the EU Cybersecurity Act, the European Union Agency for Cybersecurity contributes to EU cyber policy, enhances the trustworthiness of ICT products, services and processes with cybersecurity certification schemes, cooperates with Member States and EU bodies, and helps Europe prepare for the cyber challenges of tomorrow.

The European Union Agency for Cybersecurity considers the PCI-DSS standard a corporate governance item.

CDPSE: FOCUSED PREPARATION

Question 16.

You are the privacy solutions engineer working for a multinational healthcare organization. You are drafting a statement that is a public document which identifies who the data controller is, with contact details for its Data Protection Officer. It should also explain the purposes for which protected personal health data are collected and used, how the data are used and disclosed, how long it is kept, and the controller's legal basis for processing.
What is this statement named?

Answers:

A. Privacy Statement
B. Privacy Policy
C. Privacy Notice
D. GDPR Notice

The correct answer is C. A privacy notice is one of several documents required for GDPR compliance. However, whereas many are strictly internal, a GDPR statement is provided to customers and other interested parties, explaining how the organization processes their personal data.

Answer A is sometimes utilized in lieu of saying it is a privacy notice, however, the regulation states it is a privacy notice.

Answer B is an internal facing policy on how the organization handles and protects its data.

Answer D is incorrect.

CDPSE: FOCUSED PREPARATION

Question 17.

Your organization is a covered entity accountable to being compliant with HIPAA and your medical staff has access to all medical records within your organization. Each staff member is trained frequently on proper handling, access, and protecting of sensitive data. If one of your medical practitioners accesses an medical record in which they are not providing care to the individual associated with the record, which HIPAA rule has been violated?

Answers:

A. HITECH
B. Privacy Rule
C. Security Rule
D. Enforcement Rule

The correct answer is B. The HIPAA Privacy Rule protects the privacy of individually identifiable health information, called protected health information (PHI), as explained in the Privacy Rule. The question does not ask about ePHI or an electronic medical record. If the question had asked about an electronic form of record, the answer would be C.

CDPSE: FOCUSED PREPARATION

Question 18.

In 2009, the American Recovery and Reinvestment Act (ARRA) was signed into law by President Barack Obama. Prior to this Act, approximately only 10% of hospitals had adopted electronic health records. In order to advance healthcare, improve efficiencies and care coordination while making it easier for health information to be shared between different covered entities, electronic health records needed to be adopted.
A subsequent Act was introduced and signed into law under the ARRA to promote and expand the adoption of health information. What Act is this?

Answers:

A. Health Insurance Portability and Accountability Act
B. Health Information Exchange
C. Health Information Technology for Economic and Clinical Health Act
D. Medicare Merit-Based Incentive Program

The correct answer is C. The HITECH Act encouraged healthcare providers to adopt electronic health records and improved privacy and security protections for healthcare data. This was achieved through financial incentives for adopting EHRs and increased penalties for violations of the HIPAA Privacy and Security Rules.

CDPSE: FOCUSED PREPARATION

Question 19.

You are the privacy practitioner for an European organization. You are new to the position and are evaluating the best compliance framework that may propose to implement within your organization.
Ensuring the framework is current and applicable, you review current and past frameworks for validity, knowledge, and efficiencies.
In which chronological order were the following frameworks adopted?

Answers:

A. Directive on Privacy and Electronic Communications/Data Protection Directive/Directive on Electronic Commerce/GDPR
B. Data Protection Directive/Directive on Privacy and Electronic Communications/Directive on Electronic Commerce/GDPR
C. GDPR/Directive on Privacy and Electronic Communications/Data Protection Directive/Directive on Electronic Commerce
D. Council 108/Data Protection Directive/Directive on Electronic Commerce/Directive on Privacy and Electronic Communications

The correct answer is D. 1981, 1995, 2000, and 2002. GDPR was adopted in 2018.

CDPSE: FOCUSED PREPARATION

Question 20.

In order for you to assess a cloud provider, you must understand the cloud provider's?

Answers:

A. Privacy
B. Mission Statement
C. Notice
D. Policies

The correct answer is D. Their mission statement (answer B) is something to view and will support their policies, which will help you assess the cloud provider.

Answer A and C are not relevant to this particular question.

CDPSE: FOCUSED PREPARATION

Question 21.

Your organization is domiciled in the European Union (EU).
The third-party management program is reviewing and assessing prospective vendors to outsource certain data processing activities.
What is one topic that is not a priority for you to assess?

Answers:

A. Appropriate technical and organizational measures
B. Processor shall not engage another processor without specific or general written authorization
C. Processing by a processor shall be governed by a contract
D. What data the processor will process

The correct answer is D. What data the processor will process is not part of your assessment of the processor. That is a business decision and may assist you in narrowing your processors with their experience in processing that type of data, however, it would not be a part of your formal assessment of the vendor and their practices.

CDPSE: FOCUSED PREPARATION

Question 22.

As you and your organization review and assess prospective vendors/processors, you review data sharing implications, adequacy decisions, data subject's rights and appropriate technical and organizational measures.
Which of the following are not privacy matters to consider?

Answers:

A. Geographical location
B. Global Privacy Regulations
C. Cross-border data sharing
D. Competitor's Privacy Strategy

The correct answer is D. Although it would be nice to know what your competitors are doing, it is not a priority for your organization to focus on. The other three answers are and should be taken into consideration.

CDPSE: FOCUSED PREPARATION

Question 23.

You are the privacy solutions engineer for a U.S. based organization and are seeking new staff members for open positions. Your organization has contracted with an outside agency to collect credit reports on all applicants.
That particular vendor must provide your organization with all of the documents collected on the applicants and attest that they have provided all documents and destroyed any copies of data they collected.
Your organization has implemented a data retention policy. Based on the information provided by the Credit Reporting Agency (CRA) to your organization, your organization decides not to hire one particular individual.
After the individual discovers they were not hired due to the inaccurate information provided to the hiring organization, they may file a complaint with which agency?

Answers:

A. FCC
B. FTC
C. FDCPA
D. SNPRM

The correct answer is B. The Fair Credit Reporting Act is the primary federal law that governs the collection and reporting of credit information about consumers. Its rules cover how a consumer's credit information is obtained, how long it is kept, and how it is shared with others—including consumers themselves.

The Federal Trade Commission (FTC) and the Consumer Financial Protection Bureau (CFPB) are the two federal agencies charged with overseeing and enforcing the provisions of the act. Many states also have their own laws relating to credit reporting.

CDPSE: FOCUSED PREPARATION

Question 24.

A vendor is being assessed for future business operations and relations with your organization. Your organization will be sharing sensitive information to be processed by this vendor. You are reviewing their information risk management model and incident response plans. Your organization is required to report a known data breach within 72 hours to its regulators, however, the vendor currently reports any known data breaches within 30 days.

What type of instrument should be utilized in order to contract with this particular vendor to ensure they are compliant with your requirements?

Answers:

A. Business Associate Agreement (BAA)
B. SLA
C. MTTR
D. Legal Liability

The correct answer is A. The BAA will contain an SLA that must be understood, agreed upon and complied with by the vendor.
If the vendor agrees and signs the contract and then fails to comply, your organization may have a breach in contract terms where there may be legal ramifications and indemnifications for any losses incurred.

CDPSE: FOCUSED PREPARATION

Question 25.

As you assess your prospective vendors, what is one topic that is not a priority for you to assess?

Answers:

A. Financial
B. Geographic Location(s)
C. Privacy Framework
D. Data Inventory

The correct answer is D. Yes, you need a data inventory and will add to it once you add vendors to your vendor management portfolio, but as a prospective vendor, you do not need to focus on that, yet.

CDPSE: FOCUSED PREPARATION

Question 26.

Your organization is a covered entity and has suffered a data breach. The Office of Civil Rights has been investigating the breach and has determined your organization had a duty to your patients in protecting their data and that duty along with the data was breached, which has now caused harm or injury to your patients. What is this called?

Answers:

A. Due Care
B. Due Diligence
C. Negligence
D. Contract Law

The correct answer is C. Negligence is a tort concept available in every state, and it is broad enough to cover many types of actions. In essence, negligence is the concept that someone had a duty to someone else, the duty was breached, and the breach resulted in an injury.

CDPSE: FOCUSED PREPARATION

Question 27.

Your organization is domiciled in New Mexico. Your organization encrypts and redacts the personal and business critical data. Your organization suffers a data breach. After you have contacted your data breach coach and deploy a forensic investigator, it is determined that your encryption key has been compromised. Which law must you comply with and notify compromised data subjects?

Answers:

A. HIPAA
B. Nevada HB 15
C. New Mexico HB 15
D. New Mexico Privacy Protection Act

The correct answer is C. NM HB 15 applies to individuals, businesses, governmental entities, and other entities that own, license, or maintain personal information. The statute also has an encryption safe harbor. The statute does not apply to information that is encrypted, redacted, or otherwise rendered unreadable or unusable, as long as the encryption key is not acquired.

In this case, the encryption key has been compromised, thus nullifying the encryption safe harbor exemption.

CDPSE: FOCUSED PREPARATION

Question 28.

Your organization is domiciled in Tennessee. Your organization encrypts and redacts the personal and business critical data. Your organization suffers a data breach. After you have contacted your data breach coach and deploy a forensic investigator, it is determined that your encryption key has not been compromised. Based on your which statutory requirement will you reference to determine whether or not you must notify impacted Tennessee residents?

Answers:

A. Tennessee HB 2005
B. Tennessee SB 2005
C. Tennessee SB 2015
D. Tennessee HB 2015

The correct answer is B. Per the statute, notification of a data breach must now be provided to any affected Tennessee resident within 45-days after discovery of the breach (absent a delay request from law enforcement). Previously, and like the vast majority of states, Tennessee's statute required disclosure of a breach to be made in the most expedient time possible and without unreasonable delay.

Perhaps even more important than the specific timing requirement for notice, S.B. 2005 also amends Tennessee's statute to remove the provision in the existing statute requiring notice only in the event of a breach of unencrypted personal information.

CDPSE: FOCUSED PREPARATION

Question 29.

Your organization has suffered a data breach within your archived information. What policy will be looked at to determine whether or not your organization has complied with that policy?

Answers:

A. Acceptable Use
B. BYOD
C. Incident Response Plan
D. Retention

The correct answer is D. The key word in the question is 'archived', meaning stored and leading to the review of your retention of information.

CDPSE: FOCUSED PREPARATION

Question 30.

You are the privacy solutions engineer within your organization and are protecting the infrastructure of your organization.

With that, your teams are cleaning up programs, utilizing service packs, applying patches in accordance with your patch management program, implementing and applying group policies within the security templates, and following and updating configuration baselines.

What is your team executing?

Answers:

E. Technology review
F. System hardening
G. Security protocols
H. Secure development

The correct answer is B. System hardening processes reduce the risk of suffering a cyber-attack.

CDPSE: FOCUSED PREPARATION

Question 31.

In today's connected world, software application resiliency takes an increasingly predominant role. With the continuous discovery of new vulnerabilities in more connected systems and sensors, customers need software systems to be secure, safe, and reliable.

All of your software inventory, including new software, legacy software, open source, and/or 3rd-party software, must be protected to minimize risks of security breaches, data loss, and more.

This protective measure is done through three core techniques: software vulnerability analysis, binary patching and transformation, and software monitoring.

What is this called?

Answers:

A. System hardening
B. Application hardening
C. Software hardening
D. Threat modeling

The correct answer is C. Hardening of the OS is the act of configuring an OS securely, updating it, creating rules and policies to help govern the system in a secure manner, and removing unnecessary applications and services. This is done to minimize a computer OS's exposure to threats and to mitigate possible risk

CDPSE: FOCUSED PREPARATION

Question 32.

This infrastructure protection measure is a collection of tools, techniques, and best practices to reduce vulnerability in technology applications, systems, infrastructure, firmware, and other areas.

The goal of this action is to reduce security risk by eliminating potential attack vectors and condensing the system's attack surface. By removing superfluous programs, accounts functions, applications, ports, permissions, access, etc. attackers and malware have fewer opportunities to gain a foothold within your IT ecosystem.

What is this called?

Answers:

A. Application hardening
B. Operating system hardening
C. Server hardening
D. System hardening

The correct answer is D.

CDPSE: FOCUSED PREPARATION

Question 33.

Data privacy is a part of the data protection area that deals with the proper handling of data. This includes how data should be collected, stored and shared with any third parties, as well as compliance with the applicable privacy laws.
Data privacy is more about properly utilizing data while protecting the privacy preferences of individuals.
Data privacy is not one of these. Which one?

Answers:

A. Relationship between data collected and the individual who provided the data and the data owner
B. Public expectation of privacy
C. Is not blocking data and disposing it without use
D. Regulatory requirements to protect data

The correct answer is C.

CDPSE: FOCUSED PREPARATION

Question 34.

Access to data and devices is limited to authorized individuals, processes, and devices, and is managed consistent with the assessed risk of unauthorized access falls under which NIST Privacy Framework core function?

Answers:

A. Protect
B. Control
C. Detect
D. Identify

The correct A. The statement above is the definition of the Identify Management, Authentication and Access Control (PR.AC-P) category under the NIST Privacy Framework within the core function of Protect.

CDPSE: FOCUSED PREPARATION

Question 35.

Technical security solutions are managed to ensure the security and resilience of systems/products/services and associated data, consistent with related policies, processes, procedures, and agreements falls within which NIST Privacy Framework core function?

Answers:

A. Identify
B. Detect
C. Control
D. Protect

The correct answer is D. The statement above is the definition of the Protective Technology (PR.PT-P) category under the NIST Privacy Framework within the core function of Protect.

CDPSE: FOCUSED PREPARATION

Question 36.

You are working with procurement and legal on contracts with suppliers and third-party partners that are used to implement appropriate measures designed to meet the objectives of your organization's cybersecurity program and Cyber Supply Chain Risk Management Plan.

Which NIST framework function are you referencing for this task?

Answers:

A. Identify
B. Protect
C. Detect
D. Control

The correct answer A. The statement above is the definition of the Supply Chain Risk Management category under the NIST Cyber Security Framework within the core function of Identify.

CDPSE: FOCUSED PREPARATION

Question 37.

Access permissions and authorizations are managed, incorporating the principles of least privilege and separation of duties is part of which domain of the CDPSE outline?

Answers:

A. Privacy Governance
B. Data Cycle
C. Privacy Architecture
D. Privacy Cycle

The correct answer is C. The three domains of the CDPSE are: Privacy Governance, Privacy Architecture, and Data Cycle.

Answer D is a distractor.

CDPSE: FOCUSED PREPARATION

Question 38.

To build this process within your organization, you as the privacy solutions engineer will need a proactive and continuous approach to both privacy and cyber risk management.

This process includes embedding risk management within all business processes where customers, partners, and third-party vendors are made full-time stakeholders in your organization's process, while the business is made fully aware of all cyber risks to make better business decisions.

Answers:

A. Accountability
B. Resilience
C. Response
D. Identification

The correct answer is B.

CDPSE: FOCUSED PREPARATION

Question 39.

There are many steps and proactive measures to develop and create a cyber resilient organization. There are prioritized actions to start the resiliency program. Which one would you start with?

Answers:

A. Automation
B. Quantification
C. Security by design
D. Zero trust model

The correct answer is A. With increasing attack surfaces and new threat actors emerging, manual approaches to cyber risk management are no longer sufficient. Many enterprises are adopting AI and ML technologies to automate their assessments of risks, threats, and vulnerabilities across business-critical assets.

Answer B helps assign a specific financial amount to each identified cyber risk, signifying the actual loss that an enterprise could face. This approach helps organizations align cybersecurity with business objectives, while also optimizing cyber investments.

Answer C helps ensure that application security is not just one step in the software development lifecycle, but a checkpoint at every stage. It strengthens confidence in the inherent security of applications, so that cyber teams need worry only about high-risk and high-impact use cases when conducting in-depth assessments.

Answer D focuses on establishing user credentials, motives, and other meta-data such as location, security perimeters, and end points to determine if users can be trusted with data access. It calls for a strong governance and compliance framework to determine user access rights and authorization matrices. Privileged access rights are minimized with multi-factor authentication, identity and access management, and encryption and behavioral analytics.

CDPSE: FOCUSED PREPARATION

Question 40.

Your organization's privileged users, third-party stakeholders, senior executives and physical and cybersecurity personnel understand their roles and responsibilities due to table-top exercises and annual policy reviews.

What category do these actions fall under within the Protect function under the NIST CSF?

Answers:

A. Identify
B. Data Security
C. Awareness and Training
D. Information Protection Processes and Procedures

The correct answer is C. The organization's personnel and partners are provided cybersecurity awareness education and are trained to perform their cybersecurity- related duties and responsibilities consistent with related policies, procedures, and agreements.

Answer A is a core function, not a category.

Answer B impacts information and records (data) are managed consistent with the organization's risk strategy to protect the confidentiality, integrity, and availability of information.

Answer D addresses security policies (that address purpose, scope, roles, responsibilities, management commitment, and coordination among organizational entities), processes, and procedures are maintained and used to manage protection of information systems and assets.

CDPSE: FOCUSED PREPARATION

Question 41.

Your organization suffered a data breach, which your incident response team was able to identify, contain and respond in a timely fashion to limit the negative impact on the organization.

You are now in the recovery aspect (5th core function of the NIST CSF) and following your recovery processes and procedures are being executed and maintained to ensure restoration of systems or assets affected by the cybersecurity event.

What is your first step of the recovery process?

Answers:

A. Incorporate lessons learned
B. Update recovery strategies
C. Follow the recovery plan
D. Manage public relations and expectations

The correct answer is C.

You must follow the recovery plan to ensure efficient and effective measures are addressed in order.

CDPSE: FOCUSED PREPARATION

Question 42.

Restoration activities are coordinated with internal and external parties (e.g., coordinating centers, Internet Service Providers, owners of attacking systems, victims, other CSIRTs, and vendors).

Which NIST core function would this fall under?

Answers:

A. Recover
B. Respond
C. Communicate
D. Governance

The correct answer is A. Communications (RC.CO) falls under the Recover (RC) core function within the NIST CSF.

CDPSE: FOCUSED PREPARATION

Question 43.

Identifying everyone residing in a country, especially the poor, is an indispensable part of pursuing universal health coverage (UHC).

Some countries, such as South Korea and Thailand use this as their unique health identifier.

What is this called?

Answers:

A. National unique identification number
B. National health identification number
C. National unique health identification number
D. Civil registration

The correct answer is A. This is associated with personal data and information supporting identifying an individual.

Answer B is a distractor and incorrect.

Answer C is utilized in other countries where the unique health identifier is created in addition to the national unique identification number, but the two numbers are linked; Slovenia offers an example of this arrangement.

Answer D is a distractor and incorrect.

CDPSE: FOCUSED PREPARATION

Question 44.

You, as the privacy solutions engineer, are designing the best practices to implement within your privacy and cyber security programs.

You are enforcing least privilege access of users, conducting continuous scans, enforcing system hardening, enforcing application controls, and deploying a SIEM solution, on top of other proactive preventative measures.

What type of security are you addressing with these programs?

Answers:

A. Application security
B. Endpoint security
C. Software hardening
D. Incident response planning

The correct answer is B. You are implementing endpoint device security with those actions, securing the increasingly endpoint devices, which are becoming the main facilitator in the current Cyber threat landscape as often, internal networks are not directly reachable from the internet anymore. These internal networks are usually protected by Next-Generation Firewall Protection, while publicly available data does not reside on in-house company servers but is being accessed "in the cloud" via Content Delivery Networks (CDN's).

CDPSE: FOCUSED PREPARATION

Question 45.

You are migrating data from legacy systems to modernize your information systems. Your analysis has determined that your current information systems were never designed to quickly adapt to changing business dynamics or to address your customer's expectations.

As you develop your business case for the data migration strategy and required resources, you have determined all of the following are critical risks to address in the business case development, except?

Answers:

A. Depreciated data values
B. Security
C. Vendor solutions
D. Roll back strategy

The correct answer is C. Vendor solutions are not going to be included in the business case proposal. Once the proposal of the solution has been approved, then a potential vendor selection, RFP, may be utilized for next steps, but not for this particular case.

CDPSE: FOCUSED PREPARATION

Question 46.

As the increase in ransomware attacks (+700% since March 2020) continue to impact businesses around the world, key administrative and technical risks have been identified that are connected to those attacks being successful.

Having RDP enabled without other compensating controls in place; the lack of MFA implemented across the organization; the lack of EDR solutions and what other lacking control is a key contributor to ransomware attacks?

Answers:

A. Encryption
B. Privacy and Security Training and Awareness
C. HR Controls
D. Communications

The correct answer is B. The lack of a structured, real-time, recurring education and training program continues to be one of the key factors in allowing and enabling ransomware attacks.

CDPSE: FOCUSED PREPARATION

Question 47.

Clinical trials can have a profound impact on millions of people, but the decision to join is a very personal one. If you decide to choose to participate, you will be provided the details of the study, including possible risks and benefits, so you'll know what to expect. If you decide to participate, you'll give written permission for additional screenings and access to your health records.

What is this called when you decide to participate at this point?

Answers:

A. Written consent
B. Informed consent
C. Unambiguous consent
D. Authorization

The correct answer is B. Permission granted in the knowledge of the possible consequences, typically that which is given by a patient to a doctor for treatment with full knowledge of the possible risks and benefits is informed consent.

Answer A is when your healthcare provider recommends specific medical care, you can agree to all of it, or only some of it. Before the procedure, you'll have to complete and sign a consent form. This form is a legal document that shows your participation in the decision and your agreement to have the procedure done.

Answer C is any freely given, specific, informed and unambiguous indication of the data subject's wishes by which he or she, by a statement or by a clear affirmative action, signifies agreement to the processing of personal data relating to him or her.

Answer D is also known as precertification, is a process of reviewing certain medical, surgical or behavioral health services to ensure medical necessity and appropriateness of care prior to services being rendered.

CDPSE: FOCUSED PREPARATION

Question 48.

In December 2020, a major state-sponsored attack broke into FireEye's network and stole the company's Red Team penetration testing tools.

A few days after the announcement, a breach investigation discovered that SolarWinds Orion updates had been corrupted and weaponized by hackers.

As part of the investigation and mitigation recommendations, a key malicious domain name used in the attack had been commandeered by security experts and used as a "killswitch."

What is the definition of a "killswitch" In this situation?

Answers:

A. ...are designed to prevent your connection from accidental exposure
B. ...is a security feature that allows a data owner to remotely render a system inoperable
C. ...that the domain was reconfigured to act as a 'killswitch' that would prevent the malware from continuing to operate
D. ...is used to completely shut off a device or system

The correct answer is B. A key malicious domain name used to control potentially thousands of computer systems compromised via the months-long breach at network monitoring software vendor SolarWinds was commandeered by security experts and used as a "killswitch" designed to turn the sprawling cybercrime operation against itself.

The domain seizure was part of a collaborative effort to prevent networks that may have been affected by the compromised SolarWinds software update from communicating with the attackers. What's more, the company said the domain was reconfigured to act as a "killswitch" that would prevent the malware from continuing to operate in some circumstances.

CDPSE: FOCUSED PREPARATION

Question 49.

Cloud environments experience the same level and number of threats as do traditional data center environments. Cloud computing runs software, software has vulnerabilities, and adversaries try to exploit those vulnerabilities.

Cloud computing, responsibility for mitigating the risks that result from these software vulnerabilities is shared between the CSP and the cloud consumer.

As a result, consumers must understand the division of responsibilities and trust that the CSP meets their responsibilities. The following list of cloud-unique and shared cloud/on-premise vulnerabilities and threats were identified. Which is not a cloud-based risk?

Answers:

A. Reduced consumer visibility and control
B. On-demand self-service
C. APIs cannot be compromised
D. Unauthorized use/access

The correct answer is C. Internet-accessible management APIs CAN BE compromised. Threat actors look for vulnerabilities in management APIs. If discovered, these vulnerabilities can be turned into successful attacks, and organization cloud assets can be compromised. From there, attackers can use organization assets to perpetrate further attacks against other CSP customers.

CDPSE: FOCUSED PREPARATION

Question 50.

Which of the following is a method used to prevent SQL injection attacks?

Answers:

A. Utilizing data compression
B. Utilizing data classification
C. Utilizing parameterized database queries
D. Utilizing data warehousing

The correct answer is C. Developers can prevent SQL Injection vulnerabilities in web applications by utilizing parameterized database queries with bound, typed parameters and careful use of parameterized stored procedures in the database. This can be accomplished in a variety of programming languages including Java, . NET, PHP, and more.

CDPSE: FOCUSED PREPARATION

Question 51.

A multinational organization has decided to outsource a portion of their Information Technology organization to a third-party provider's facility.

This provider will be responsible for the design, development, testing, and support of several critical, customer- based applications used by the organization.

The third party needs to have?

Answers:

A. Processes that are identical to that of the organization doing the outsourcing
B. Access to the original personnel that were on staff at the organization
C. The ability to maintain all of the applications in languages they are familiar with
D. Access to the skill sets consistent with the programming languages used by the organization

The correct answer is D.

CDPSE: FOCUSED PREPARATION

Question 52.

Which one of the following is a threat related to the use of web-based client-side input validation?

Answers:

A. The web server would not be able to validate the input after transmission
B. The client system could receive invalid input from the web server
C. Users would be able to alter the input after validation has occurred
D. The web server would not be able to receive invalid input from the client

The correct answer is C.

CDPSE: FOCUSED PREPARATION

Question 53.

Which of the following is a security limitation of File Transfer Protocol (FTP)?

Answers:

A. Authentication is not encrypted
B. Passive FTP is not compatible with web browsers
C. Anonymous access is allowed
D. FTP uses Transmission Control Protocol (TCP) ports 20 and 21

The correct answer is A.

CDPSE: FOCUSED PREPARATION

Question 54.

In Disaster Recovery (DR) and business continuity training, which BEST describes a functional rehearsal?

Answers:

A. A full-scale simulation of an emergency and the subsequent response functions
B. A functional evacuation of personnel
C. An activation of the backup site
D. A specific test by response teams of individual emergency response functions

The correct answer is D.

CDPSE: FOCUSED PREPARATION

Question 55.

A vulnerability in which of the following components would be MOST difficult to detect?

Answers:

A. Kernel
B. Shared libraries
C. Hardware
D. System application

The correct answer is A.

CDPSE: FOCUSED PREPARATION

Question 56.

Which of the following is not a response to a prepared security assessment report that you created with your assessment of your organization's risk posture?

Answers:

A. Transfer of risk
B. Transfer of acceptance of risk
C. Share risk
D. Accept risk

The correct answer is B.

Risk responses are Accept, Avoid, Mitigate, Share and Transfer risk.

If a risk is to be shared, the parties that agree to share the risk then must make a formal decision on what risk response they will take – Accept, Avoid, Mitigate or Transfer.

CDPSE: FOCUSED PREPARATION

Question 57.

A Denial of Service (DoS) attack on a syslog server exploits weakness in which of the following protocols?

Answers:

A. Point-to-Point Protocol (PPP) and Internet Control Message Protocol (ICMP)
B. Address Resolution Protocol (ARP) and Reverse Address Resolution Protocol (RARP)
C. Transmission Control Protocol (TCP) and User Datagram Protocol (UDP)
D. Transport Layer Security (TLS) and Secure Sockets Layer (SSL)

The correct answer is C.

CDPSE: FOCUSED PREPARATION

Question 58.

In a data classification scheme, the data is owned by the?

Answers:

A. Business Managers
B. Privacy Officer
C. Legal
D. Users

The correct answer is A.

CDPSE: FOCUSED PREPARATION

Question 59.

Medical records are the document that explains all details about the patient's history, clinical findings, diagnostic test results, pre and postoperative care, patient's progress and medication.

Management of those records is the part of records management that relates to the operation of a healthcare practice. It is the field of management that is responsible for all records throughout their lifecycle from creation, receipt, maintenance, and use to disposal.

As part of this management program, a U.S. based healthcare organization must retain those records for how long?

Answers:

A. 5 years
B. 6 years
C. 7 years
D. 10 years

The correct answer is B. The Health Insurance Portability and Accountability Act (HIPAA) of 1996 (HIPAA) administrative simplification rules require a covered entity, such as a physician billing Medicare, to retain required documentation for six years from the date of its creation or the date when it last was in effect, whichever is later.

CDPSE: FOCUSED PREPARATION

Question 60.

HR is reviewing candidate's resumes and background information based on an open job posting. What is one risk area that you, as the privacy solutions engineer, should work with Legal and HR on, as it relates to the background information gathered?

Answers:

A. Data Retention
B. Data Policies
C. Information
D. Training

The correct answer is A. Data retention, not only at the controller's location, but also within the contract with the processor who is obtaining the background information.

The controller must be explicit with what the processor will do with the information gathered on the individual once a decision has been executed on hiring or not hiring of the candidate. Based on that decision, both the controller and processor must retain and then destroy the data that is no longer required for any business reason.

CDPSE: FOCUSED PREPARATION

Question 61.

Your organization has completed their regulatory mapping exercise and determined and created their data retention policy. The institution has adopted two possible standards for destroying the data, which are degaussing and shredding. What is another way to destroy the data electronically?

Answers:

A. Melt
B. Burn
C. Erase
D. Overwrite

The correct answer is D. Answer A and B are physical, not electronic destruction methods. Answer C is a synonym for degaussing.

CDPSE: FOCUSED PREPARATION

Question 62.

Your organization, a covered entity within the U.S., has suffered a data breach within your archived information. What policy will be looked at to determine whether or not your organization has complied with that policy?

Answers:

A. Acceptable Use
B. BYOD
C. Incident Response Plan
D. Retention

The correct answer is D. The key word in the question is 'archived', meaning stored and leading to the review of your retention of information.

CDPSE: FOCUSED PREPARATION

Question 63.

A California, U.S. based organization receives its first subject access request (SAR). The privacy officer is alerted to receipt of the request in a timely fashion. What document will be referenced, that was developed in the establishment of the privacy program, that will assist in determining where the SAR's information resides?

Answers:

A. Data Classification Policy
B. Privacy Program Scope
C. Regulatory Map
D. Data Inventory

The correct answer is D. The data inventory will provide the PPM with the source, types, uses, information flow path, storage, and other applicable data fields to start the collection of the SAR form.

CDPSE: FOCUSED PREPARATION

Question 64.

A global multi-diversified organization located in numerous countries would be best to implement this type of governance model?

Answers:

A. Centralized
B. Distributed
C. Hybrid
D. External

The correct answer is B. Distributed delegates decision-making to the lowest levels within an organization allowing a bottom-to-top flow of decisions and monitoring.

CDPSE: FOCUSED PREPARATION

Question 65.

Your global financial organization is structuring your privacy team. Which privacy domain houses this action item?

Answers:

A. Measure
B. Improve
C. Privacy Program Framework
D. Developing a Privacy Program

The correct answer is D. When your organization is developing the privacy program, they will create the company vision, establish a data governance model, establish a privacy program, structure the privacy team and communicate, both internally and externally pertaining to their accountability.

CDPSE: FOCUSED PREPARATION

Question 66.

An international organization is implementing their privacy program. While they are in that process, they are conducting self-assessments, developing procedures, communicating and monitoring the program. What type of management is this called?

Answers:

A. Information Security Management System
B. Risk Management
C. Centralized Management
D. Information Management

The correct answer is D.

Answer A is a security management system.

Answer B is incorrect.

Answer C is a governance model. Information management consists of discovering, building, communicating, and growth.

CDPSE: FOCUSED PREPARATION

Question 67.

As privacy laws and regulations continue to expand and change, complying and monitoring with those changes is critical for your organization's privacy program success. What is one solution that provides organizations with updated changes, monitoring and auditing performances of their processes and procedures?

Answers:

A. Internal Audit
B. Second-party Audit
C. Third-party Audit
D. Third-party Privacy Compliance Platform and Tools

The correct answer is D. 3rd party external resources and tools provide organizations of any size with real-time legal and regulatory changes, particular audits and process compliance, along with baseline measures based on industry vertical and other criteria.

CDPSE: FOCUSED PREPARATION

Question 68.

Prior to a new service or system being implemented in your international organization, this type of action is required to be conducted?

Answers:

A. Data Privacy Impact Assessment
B. Privacy Impact Assessment
C. Privacy Assessment
D. Risk Assessment

The correct answer is B. Privacy Impact Assessment is an assessment of the privacy risks identified with processing of personal information in connection with a product, project or service.

Answer A, Data Protection Impact Assessment must be conducted to identify risks when processing personal data and is required within the GDPR.

Answer C, Privacy Assessment, measured an organization's compliance to legal and regulatory requirements, policies and processes and standards.

Answer D, Risk Assessment, could be an assessment of any processes, that may or may not impact privacy or data protection.

CDPSE: FOCUSED PREPARATION

Question 69.

Your organization is capturing and documenting where and what information is flowing, both internally and externally. What is this type of exercise?

Answers:

A. Regulatory Map
B. Legal Map
C. Data Inventory Map
D. Data Map

The correct answer is C.

Answers A and B are to determine regulatory and legal requirements that your organization is accountable to and for.

Answer D is the process of matching fields from one database to another.

CDPSE: FOCUSED PREPARATION

Question 70.

What is one risk area that you, as the privacy solutions engineer, should focus on, as it relates to a vendor gathering sensitive information from your organization is what?

Answers:

A. Procurement
B. Vendor Assessment
C. Information Risk
D. Communications

The correct answer is B. The organization, prior to signing any contracts with a particular vendor, must assess the prospective vendor based on the organization's standards and regulatory requirements that must be complied with by the processor.

CDPSE: FOCUSED PREPARATION

Question 71.

What must an efficient and successful privacy program within an organization be built with?

Answers:

A. Data Map
B. Regulatory Map
C. Compliance Map
D. Comprehensive View

The correct answer is D.

Answers A and B are components of the comprehensive view within the organization. Each organization must know what data that collects and processes throughout the data's entire lifecycle.

CDPSE: FOCUSED PREPARATION

Question 72.

Your organization completed the data inventory exercise. Who in your organization determines what classifications of information are arranged into those categories?

Answers:

A. Chief Security Officer
B. Chief Executive Officer
C. Privacy Officer
D. Human Resources

The correct answer is C. The Privacy Officer and legal department review all regulatory and legal requirements of the organization and based on those applicable laws, will determine what classifications will be utilized within the organization.

Answer A will overlay the appropriate physical, administrative and technical controls, based on those categories of data.

Answer B and D are not the correct answers.

CDPSE: FOCUSED PREPARATION

Question 73.

Your multinational organization is acquiring another multinational organization. As part of the privacy checkpoint, your organization's processes should consist of conducting a _____ prior to the integration of the acquired organization's systems and processes.

Answers:

A. Divestiture
B. Data inventory
C. Regulatory map
D. Risk Assessment

The correct answer is D. A risk assessment of the acquired organization's systems, processes, and technologies should be conducted prior to integrating systems to your organization's systems. This will identify potential risks and allow time to mitigate those while protecting and not introducing those new risks to your organization.

CDPSE: FOCUSED PREPARATION

Question 74.

Your organization is capturing and documenting where and what information is flowing, both internally and externally. What does the end product assist your organization with?

Answers:

A. Identifies vendors
B. Identifies regulatory requirements
C. Identifies classification
D. Identifies personal information use

The correct answer is D.

A data inventory will identify the source, types and uses of personal information.

Answer A and B could be an answer, but not with the limited information provided.

Answer C would be a by-product of the identification of the personal use information.

CDPSE: FOCUSED PREPARATION

Question 75.

One of the goals that is not one of the privacy solution engineer's roles is to?

Answers:

A. To identify their supply chain's privacy risks.
B. To identify their organizations, employees, and customer's risks.
C. To identify current state of policies, procedures, and any supporting documentation.
D. Promote consumer trust.

The correct answer is A. The engineer's goal is not to identify their supply chain's privacy risks. That would be a part of the Vendor Management program.

Answer B and C are a few of the goals of the privacy solution engineer.

Answer D is a goal of the privacy program, which, ultimately, is an implied goal of the privacy practitioner, not the engineer. The best correct answer is A.

CDPSE: FOCUSED PREPARATION

Question 76.

Which of the following groups are not a priority group for the development of your privacy policies and procedures within your organization?

Answers:

A. Human Resources
B. Legal
C. Business Development
D. External Audit

The correct answer is D. An internal audit group would be a part of your priority group. All of the other groups are departments you should include.

CDPSE: FOCUSED PREPARATION

Question 77.

A multinational organization's privacy program maturity level is based on how established the program is functioning in multiple areas. Generally, if your privacy program has recently been created where you are still evaluating and inventorying what the organization has and does not have in place for policies, processes and procedures, the privacy program maturity level is at this stage?

Answers:

A. Repeatable
B. Defined
C. Ad Hoc
D. Managed

The correct answer is C. Ad Hoc levels are informal, incomplete and inconsistently implemented. It is the initial maturity level.

CDPSE: FOCUSED PREPARATION

Question 78.

Once the policies, procedures and security controls have been assessed on your potential cloud provider, whom within your organization should approve of this type of vendor?

Answers:

A. General Counsel
B. Privacy Program Manager
C. Chief Information Security Officer
D. Chief Information Officer

The correct answer is D. All listed answers may be involved with the business case development, screening criteria of the vendor and review of the vendor, however, since it is a technical vendor, a cloud provider, ultimately, the CIO should approve of the provider.

CDPSE: FOCUSED PREPARATION

Question 79.

Your multinational organization processes and collects over 1,000,000 credit card transactions annually.
You collect credit card transactions at a kiosk and registration desk for all in-coming patients.
You collect credit card transactions in the café, gift shop, and pharmacy, as well.
You have conducted an assessment on your PCI-DSS compliance. The PCI-DSS deals strictly with payment card data and cardholder information, such as credit/debit card numbers, primary account numbers (PAN), and sensitive authentication data (SAD) such as CVVs and magnetic stripe data, from all the major card schemes.

The GDPR has a much wider scope and covers any personally identifiable information (PII). The type of data in scope for GDPR includes PII related to any EU resident, whether it is connected to his or her private, professional or public life. This can include a name, home address, photo, email address, bank details, medical information, posts on social networking websites, or a computer's IP address.
Your organization suffers a breach that violates PCI DSS compliance, which now, also, violates the GDPR.
Which data protection principle applies here?

Answers:

A. Data minimization
B. Integrity and Confidentiality
C. Storage limitation
D. Purpose limitation

The correct answer is B. The PCI-DSS establishes a set of controls for keeping cardholder data secure, supported by a regulatory framework. If deployed to the rest of the business – without extending the cardholder data environment – these same controls and processes could provide organizations with a head start in meeting the sixth principle of the GDPR (integrity and confidentiality). This principle requires data controllers and processors to assess risk, implement appropriate security for the data concerned and, crucially, check on a regular basis that it is up to date and that controls to protect it are working effectively.

CDPSE: FOCUSED PREPARATION

Question 80.

Your organization is outsourcing its account management program.

When this happens, what type of service are you requesting?

Answers:

A. Platform as a Service (PaaS)
B. Desktop as a Service (DaaS)
C. Identity as a Service (IDaaS)
D. Software as a Service (SaaS)

The correct answer is C.

CDPSE: FOCUSED PREPARATION

Question 81.

An organization that suffers a cyber event may be investigated to determine if they had the appropriate policies and procedures in place, along with documented training for their workforce. If the organization had those correct controls in place, this organization is able to prove that they have?

Answers:

A. Consumer Trust
B. Compliance
C. Accountability
D. Responsibility

The best, correct answer would be C. Accountability. Accountable organizations will be able to show tangible evidence that they have executed both their due care and due diligence as it relates to policy development, implementation, dissemination, training, and follow-up actions ensuring that their workforce is able to apply and comply with those policies and procedures. Consumer trust (Answer A) is a by-product of being accountable, as is Compliance (Answer B). The organization is being responsible (Answer D) by being accountable. Without being accountable, the organization would not have trust. The organization would more than likely not be compliant, nor would they be responsible in protecting their data.

CDPSE: FOCUSED PREPARATION

Question 82.

You have set up your data warehouse to be read-only by default. This prevents any dangerous SQL write statements from being executed on your data.

What is this called?

Answers:

A. Slave read-only
B. Data encryption
C. Custom user group development
D. BI tool implementation

The correct answer is A.

CDPSE: FOCUSED PREPARATION

Question 83.

As your organization plans its transition from a data lake to a data warehouse solution, there are a number of proactive preventative steps your organization will need to take into consideration to protect the confidentiality of the data.

Understanding that more groups, more people and possibly more systems will have access to this data, your organization will need to identify what data characteristics are stored in the warehouse, to include PII, financial information, sensitive data, etc.

You need to ensure that sensitive information is aligned to what is being stored, how it's restricted in the data warehouse, and how it can be accessed via your BI tools.

What is the most direct way to limit access to the data?

Answers:

A. Custom user groups
B. Role-based access
C. Slave read-only
D. Enforce rules at database level

The correct answer is D. This can be executed through creating slave read-only replicas, creating of custom user groups, and encrypting sensitive data.

CDPSE: FOCUSED PREPARATION

Question 84.

You have implemented Identifying, Governing, Controlling, Communicating, and Protecting functional controls to assist in protecting the privacy of your organization's data.

Which of these functional core controls addresses disassociated processing?

Answers:

A. Identify
B. Control
C. Protect
D. Govern

The correct answer is B. The NIST Privacy Framework installs those five functional core services to assist in protecting the privacy of data.

The Control core function addresses disassociated processing. Data processing solutions increase dissociable consistent with the organization's risk strategy to protect individuals' privacy and enable implementation of privacy principles (e.g., data minimization).

CDPSE: FOCUSED PREPARATION

Question 85.

Your businesses must know what their Location Based Service (LBS) does, what type of data it collects and whether that data is shared with affiliates, partners or third parties.

A number of critical threats posed to the privacy of individuals stemming from LBS services is the unintended revelation of a user's home address, and websites demonstrating the danger of location-sharing by providing a database of empty homes based on users' "check-ins" elsewhere.

While these may be some of the more extreme examples, it is not uncommon for some LBS-enabled popular services to omit clear disclosures about the extent to which personal information is collected from the consumer and how it is used and have a process that obtains informed consumer consent for such data collection.

How should you conduct threat analysis on LBS services?

Answers:

A. Conduct threat modeling
B. Vulnerability assessments
C. Conduct location assessments
D. Turn of LBS services

The correct answer is A. Threat modeling is a structured process through which privacy solutions engineers can identify potential security threats and vulnerabilities, quantify the seriousness of each, and prioritize techniques to mitigate attack and protect resources.

Those actions will allow you to analyze the known threats and devise a strategy to reduce the likelihood of those threats exploiting any vulnerabilities to the LBS services.

CDPSE: FOCUSED PREPARATION

Question 86.

In this type of threat, the attacker can receive continuous updates of user location in real time, which can be used to identify the user's location routes, predict future locations, and/or frequently traveled routes with sufficient accuracy using a user's mobility patterns.

What type of threat is this called?

Answers:

A. Identification threat
B. Profiling threat
C. Tracking threat
D. Data threat

The correct answer is C.

Answer A is a type of threat the attacker can receive sporadic updates of user location, which can be used to identify the user's frequently visited locations (such as home or workplace) and these places can be used to disclose a user's identity.

Answer B is a type of threat the attacker may not have the required information to identify the user but can use the locations to profile the user. For example, an attacker can identify which hospitals or religious places a user visits, or which places the user goes for shopping, and how often.

CDPSE: FOCUSED PREPARATION

Question 87.

Your technology organization is finalizing both the privacy policy and the information security policy. They are both drastically different, to include the structure to how they are presented and available for consumption.

They are both presented in with a layered approach. One of them is defining three levels. The top layer is a high-level document containing the controller's policy statement. The next layer is a more detailed document that sets out the security controls that will be implemented to achieve the policy statements. The third layer is the most detailed and contains the operating procedures, which explain how the policy statements will be achieved in practice.

Which policy are we discussing?

Answers:

A. Privacy Policy
B. Information Security Policy
C. Integrity Policy
D. Privacy Notice (layered)

The correct answer is B. The key word is in the second layer description. The security controls that will be implemented.
This question is not trying to trick you. It is to help you focus on key words in the question that are being posed for you to pick up on.

You will have questions that will be vague, however, there will be a key word or term within it that will help you.

CDPSE: FOCUSED PREPARATION

Question 88.

A publicly traded company and its cybersecurity protection is critical to your operations. The impact of a successful cyber-attack may have consequences that extend beyond your organization and impacts other market participants and retail investors, who may not be well informed of these risks and consequences.

What organization continues to prioritize cybersecurity in each of its five examination programs that focus on, among other things, proper configuration of network storage devices, information security governance generally, and policies and procedures related to retail trading information security.

Specific to investment advisers, what organization emphasizes cybersecurity practices at investment advisers with multiple branch offices, including those that have recently merged with other investment advisers, and continue to focus on, among other areas, governance and risk assessment, access rights and controls, data loss prevention, vendor management, training, and incident response?

Answers:

A. National Labor Relations Board
B. Occupational Safety and Health Act
C. Office of Compliance Inspections and Examinations
D. Department of Labor

The correct answer is C. The Office of Compliance Inspections and Examinations (OCIE) falls under the U.S. Securities and Exchange Commission (SEC). The initial sentence identifies your organization as a publicly traded company.

With approximately 1,000 staff in the Commission's 11 regional offices and headquarters, OCIE is responsible for overseeing the Financial Industry Regulatory Authority (FINRA), the Municipal Securities Rulemaking Board (MSRB), the Securities Investor Protection Corporation, and the Public Company Accounting Oversight Board.

CDPSE: FOCUSED PREPARATION

Question 89.

When a web server sends an HTML file to a client, it uses the hypertext transfer protocol (HTTP) to do so. The HTTP program layer asks this layer to set up the connection and send the file.

Although each packet in the transmission has the same source and destination IP address, packets may be sent along multiple routes.

Which communication protocol is this?

Answers:

A. HTTP
B. DNS
C. Network Layer
D. TCP

The correct answer is D. TCP (Transmission Control Protocol) is a standard that defines how to establish and maintain a network conversation through which application programs can exchange data. TCP works with the Internet Protocol (IP), which defines how computers send packets of data to each other. Together, TCP and IP are the basic rules defining the Internet. The Internet Engineering Task Force (IETF) defines TCP in the Request for Comment (RFC) standards document number 793.

CDPSE: FOCUSED PREPARATION

Question 90.

Your organization operates a commercial website and online services that collect and maintain covered information from all of its consumers. Your organization is targeting a number of states and their residents. Which one of these states must you be compliant with their website privacy notification law?

Answers:

A. Minnesota
B. Colorado
C. Washington
D. Nevada

The correct answer is D. Nevada's new law follows in the footsteps of laws passed in California (2004) and Delaware (2016) requiring similar notices from any commercial website that collects personally identifiable information from the states' residents. Nevada's new law, though, is more limited in its application—it applies only if the owners or operators of a commercial website or service purposefully direct or conduct activities in Nevada or consummate some transaction with the state or one of its residents.

CDPSE: FOCUSED PREPARATION

Question 91.

Under the Fair and Accurate Credit Transaction Act (FACTA) organization's goals are all of these except:

Answers:

A. Notification
B. Prevention
C. Detection
D. Mitigation of identity theft

The correct answer is A.

CDPSE: FOCUSED PREPARATION

Question 92.

Your organization, a private entity based in Illinois, captures biometric data for providing secure building access, tracking employee time and attendance, and authenticating users' identities for increased computer and mobile device login security.
Your organization has provided notice to the employees, obtained written consent and made certain disclosures.

What other requirement is needed by this organization?

Answers:

A. Develop a privacy notice
B. Develop the privacy program strategy
C. Develop a written HR policy
D. Develop a retention schedule

The correct answer is D. Organizations are required to develop a written policy establishing a retention schedule and guidelines for permanently destroying biometric data, under Illinois' Biometric Information Privacy Act (BIPA).

Answer A is for consumers, not employees.

CDPSE: FOCUSED PREPARATION

Question 93.

The Fair and Accurate Credit Transactions Act (FACTA) adds provisions designed to promote data accuracy, fairness and privacy of information within the files of consumer reporting agencies. One requirement financial organizations must develop and implement are methods of detecting identity theft. What mandate is this called?

A.   Fair Credit Reporting Act (FCRA)
B.   Federal Trade Commission (FTC)
C.   Red Flags Rule
D.   Protective Order

The best, correct answer is C. Red Flags Rule.

Answer A allows consumers a free credit report every twelve months. Answer B is the authoritative body which governs the FCRA and FACTA. Answer D is a ruling in which information should not be made public and applies constraints to who shall have access to this protected information

These types of questions, with that thought process, are highly likely to be presented to you on your exam.

CDPSE: FOCUSED PREPARATION

Question 94.

The Transactions and Code Sets standard within HIPAA was created to standardize the electronic exchange of patient-identifiable, health-related information.

It is based on electronic data interchange (EDI) standards, which allow the electronic exchange of information from computer to computer without human involvement.

How best would you integrate data within your business as the privacy solutions engineer?

Answers:

A. Conduct data inventory
B. Review asset management inventory
C. Conduct information data flow exercise
D. Outsource the solution

The correct answer is B.

For most EDI systems, the greatest development task is integrating EDI systems with existing corporate applications. You must review your asset inventory to determine those corporate applications and then review the data flow map, both internally and externally flowing data.

Data required by trading partners and EDI standards must be "mapped" onto data contained in existing systems.

CDPSE: FOCUSED PREPARATION

Question 95.

This HIPAA Rule requires covered entities to notify affected individuals; HHS; and, in some cases, the media of a breach of unsecured PHI.

This rule also requires business associates of covered entities to notify the covered entity of breaches at or by the business associate.

Answers:

A. Privacy Rule
B. Security Rule
C. Enforcement Rule
D. Breach Notification Rule

The correct answer is D.

Answer A protects all "individually identifiable health information" held or transmitted by a covered entity or its business associate, in any form or media, whether electronic, paper, or oral. The Privacy Rule calls this information "protected health information (PHI)."

Answer B establishes national standards to protect individuals' electronic personal health information that is created, received, used, or maintained by a covered entity.

Answer C establishes how HHS regulators will determine liability and calculate fines for health-care providers found to have violated any of the HIPAA rules following an investigation and administrative hearing.

CDPSE: FOCUSED PREPARATION

Question 96.

All 50 states, the District of Columbia (D.C), Puerto Rico and the U.S. Virgin Islands all have state data breach notification laws. Each state law varies, however, share the same basic elements. All of the following states include biometric data within their data breach laws, except:

Answers:

A. CT
B. MN
C. WI
D. NM

The correct answer is B.

CT, IL, IA, NE, NM, NC, OR, WI and WY all include unique biometric data within their state data breach laws.

CDPSE: FOCUSED PREPARATION

Question 97.

Your organization is domiciled in Tennessee. Your organization encrypts and redacts the personal and business critical data. Your organization suffers a data breach. After you have contacted your data breach coach and deploy a forensic investigator, it is determined that your encryption key has not been compromised. Based on statutory requirements, how soon must you notify affected Tennessee residents of the data breach?

Answers:

A. 15 Days
B. 30 Days
C. 45 Days
D. 60 Days

The correct answer is C. Per the statute, notification of a data breach must now be provided to any affected Tennessee resident within 45-days after discovery of the breach (absent a delay request from law enforcement). Previously, and like the vast majority of states, Tennessee's statute required disclosure of a breach to be made in the most expedient time possible and without unreasonable delay.

CDPSE: FOCUSED PREPARATION

Question 98.

Consumer Online Privacy Rights Act (COPRA) and the United States Consumer Data Privacy Act (USCDPA) drafts are both addressing a key individual right.

The USCDPA contains no provision for this right. COPRA does have one (Section 301(c)), and it allows for all forms of relief within its draft. What right is being discussed?

Answers:

A. Class-action
B. Liability
C. Private Right of Action
D. Privacy Act

The correct answer is C. A private right of action allows individuals aggrieved by violations of the law to file lawsuits against violators in order to obtain money damages in federal court.

CDPSE: FOCUSED PREPARATION

Question 99.

Your organization encrypts and redacts the personal and business critical data it controls. Your organization suffers a data breach. After you have contacted your data breach coach and deploy a forensic investigator, it is determined that your encryption key has not been compromised. Based on Art. 33, who must you notify?

Answers:

A. Data Protection Authority
B. Supervisory Authority
C. Data Protection Officer
D. No one

The correct answer is D. A notification to a supervisory authority is not required if there is unlikely to be a risk to the rights and freedoms of individuals. The WP gives an example of where a securely encrypted mobile device is lost but the organization retains the encryption key and adequate backup copies of the lost data.

If the encryption key is compromised, the controller shall without undue delay and, where feasible, not later than 72 hours after having become aware of it notify the supervisory authority.

CDPSE: FOCUSED PREPARATION

Question 100.

You, a citizen of a Member State, discovers and confirms that your information that is stored with a telecom organization (controller) is incorrect. Which GDPR article provides you the right to rectify that discrepancy?

Answers:

A. Art. 16
B. Art. 15
C. Art. 17
D. Art. 19

The correct answer is A.

Chapter 3 (Art. 12 – 23) Rights of the data subject

Art. 12 Transparent information, communication and modalities for the exercise of the rights of the data subject
Art. 13 Information to be provided where personal data are collected from the data subject
Art. 14 Information to be provided where personal data have not been obtained from the data subject
Art. 15 Right of access by the data subject
Art. 16 Right to rectification
Art. 17 Right to erasure ('right to be forgotten')
Art. 18 Right to restriction of processing
Art. 19 Notification obligation regarding rectification or erasure of personal data or restriction of processing

CDPSE: FOCUSED PREPARATION

Question 101.

The objective of this process is to assess an organization's privacy protection posture against any legislative/regulatory requirements or international best practices and to review compliance with the organization's own privacy-related policies.

The scope involves evaluating procedures undertaken by an organization throughout the typical information life-cycle phases: how information is created or received, distributed, used, maintained and eventually disposed of. As information and data have transformed from being scarce to superabundant, this process presents the status of risk associated with potential information misuse and recommends initiatives that can limit an organization's liability or reputational risk.

What is this process called?

Answers:

A. Privacy notice
B. Privacy impact assessment
C. Privacy audit process
D. Privacy risk assessment

The correct answer is C.

The privacy audit methodology includes:
- Establish context
- Identify privacy risk
- Analyze privacy risk
- Evaluate privacy risk
- Manage privacy risk
- Communicate and consult
- Monitor and review

CDPSE: FOCUSED PREPARATION

Question 102.

This is a standard that embodies many principles of interoperable and secure software for electronic health records. This work aims to understand to what extent the standard can be considered a solution for the requirements needed by GDPR.

What standard is this called?

Answers:

A. Electronic Health Record
B. Electronic Medical Record
C. OpenEHR
D. Privacy Standard

The correct answer is C.

Answer A and B are often interchanged and may include your medical history, notes, and other information about your health including your symptoms, diagnoses, medications, lab results, vital signs, immunizations, and reports from diagnostic tests such as x-rays.

Answer D is a distractor and incorrect.

CDPSE: FOCUSED PREPARATION

Question 103.

The Coronavirus has impacted the globe both personally and professionally. Initial reports in March and April 2020 had five new cases a day being reported in areas, which was viewed as high. On November 4, 2020, over 100k cases were reported in one day within the U.S.
You are responsible for protecting the collection and reporting of this data within your privacy solutions engineer role.
What type of processing of personal data is this?

Answers:

A. Legitimate Interest
B. Public Interest
C. Consent
D. Contract

The correct answer is B. According to Article 9 (2) of the GDPR, sensitive data, including personal health-related data, can only be processed inter alia when data subject gives her/his explicit consent or when processing is necessary 'for reasons of public interest in the area of public health' on the basis of Union or Member State law.

CDPSE: FOCUSED PREPARATION

Question 104.

The Directive on Patients' Rights in Cross-Border Healthcare provides a legal basis for establishing a network on e-health in order to address such practical issues, focusing in particular on cross-border aspects (such as summary records for cross-border care, identification and secure sharing of information), as well as the vital strategic issue of methods for using e-health to enable use of medical information for public health and research – potentially an answer to address the delays that currently plague health data.

The European Commission also finances a wide range of projects developing and piloting e-health technologies and applications, for example in support of the European Innovation Partnership on Active and Healthy Ageing. E-health is presented as a way to address the shortage of health professionals in the European Union, to ensure better care of ageing populations and chronic diseases putting pressure on health budgets, as well as to remedy unequal quality and access to healthcare services in Europe.
Which Article of the GDPR addresses personal health information?

Answers:

A. Art. 4
B. Art. 5
C. Art. 9
D. Art. 11

The correct answer is C. Article 9, Processing of special categories of personal data is processing of personal data revealing racial or ethnic origin, political opinions, religious or philosophical beliefs, or trade union membership, and the processing of genetic data, biometric data for the purpose of uniquely identifying a natural person, data concerning health or data concerning a natural person's sex life or sexual orientation shall be prohibited.

CDPSE: FOCUSED PREPARATION

Question 105.

An individual is applying for a new, open position listed on a job board website for your organization.

The application contains multiple 'yes or no' health-related questions. The application's Health History section states in large letters that "All questions must be answered before we can process your application."

The individual did not answer the questions based on their medical condition and disabilities due to had they have answered, they would have revealed those conditions and disabilities. Which Act is being violated here?

Answers:

A. Americans with Disabilities Act
B. EEOC
C. OSHA
D. National Labor Act

The correct answer is A. The ADA is a civil rights law that prohibits discrimination against individuals with disabilities in all areas of public life, including jobs, schools, transportation, and all public and private places that are open to the general public. The purpose of the law is to make sure that people with disabilities have the same rights and opportunities as everyone else.
The ADA gives civil rights protections to individuals with disabilities similar to those provided to individuals on the basis of race, color, sex, national origin, age, and religion. It guarantees equal opportunity for individuals with disabilities in public accommodations, employment, transportation, state and local government services, and telecommunications. The ADA is divided into five titles (or sections) that relate to different areas of public life.

CDPSE: FOCUSED PREPARATION

Question 106.

The CFO and CHR of a manufacturing organization are looking to you, the privacy solutions engineer, to provide them with a performance measurement of the privacy protection program. Which of the following would you not utilize in creating that?

Answers:

A. Tracking
B. Identifying
C. Defining
D. Analyzing

The correct answer is B. The audience is already identified within the question. The other answers would all be utilized to create the performance measurement report.

CDPSE: FOCUSED PREPARATION

Question 107.

The FBI, HHS-OIG, and CMS have received complaints of scammers using the public's interest in COVID-19 vaccines to obtain personally identifiable information (PII) and money through various schemes.

The public should be aware of the following potential indicators of fraudulent activity:

- Advertisements or offers for early access to a vaccine upon payment of a deposit or fee
- Requests asking you to pay out of pocket to obtain the vaccine or to put your name on a COVID-19 vaccine waiting list
- Offers to undergo additional medical testing or procedures when obtaining a vaccine
- Marketers offering to sell and/or ship doses of a vaccine, domestically or internationally, in exchange for payment of a deposit or fee
- Unsolicited emails, telephone calls, or personal contact from someone claiming to be from a medical office, insurance company, or COVID-19 vaccine center requesting personal and/or medical information to determine recipients' eligibility to participate in clinical vaccine trials or obtain the vaccine
- Claims of FDA approval for a vaccine that cannot be verified
- Advertisements for vaccines through social media platforms, email, telephone calls, online, or from unsolicited/unknown sources
- Individuals contacting you in person, by phone, or by email to tell you the government or government officials require you to receive a COVID-19 vaccine

How can you as the privacy solutions engineer preempt both your organization's data and your patient's data from being compromised?

Answers:

A. Training and Awareness outreach programs
B. Privacy notice
C. Encryption
D. Role based access

The correct answer is A. Other prevention techniques are:
- Verify the spelling of web addresses, websites, and email addresses that look trustworthy but may be imitations of legitimate websites.
- Ensure operating systems and applications are updated to the most current versions.
- Update anti-malware and anti-virus software and conduct regular network scans.
- Do not enable macros on documents downloaded from an email unless necessary and after ensuring the file is not malicious.
- Do not communicate with or open emails, attachments, or links from unknown individuals.

CDPSE: FOCUSED PREPARATION

- Never provide personal information of any sort via email; be aware that many emails requesting your personal information may appear to be legitimate.
- Use strong two-factor authentication if possible, using biometrics, hardware tokens, or authentication apps.
- Disable or remove unneeded software applications.
- Answer C is a distracting and incorrect answer.

CDPSE: FOCUSED PREPARATION

Question 108.

Your multinational organization is migrating their applications and processes to a cloud computing platform.
Accessibility, storage and management are key business drivers for this effort.

All of the following are challenges in cloud computing within GDPR except?

Answers:

A. Data retention
B. Data processing outside of the EEA
C. Data ownership
D. Vendor management

The correct answer is D. All of the other answers are correct. Vendor management is not a part of cloud computing, however, selecting a vendor for cloud computing may be a challenge, but that is not what the question is asking you.

You will see questions similar to this ask and thought process on your exam.

CDPSE: FOCUSED PREPARATION

Question 109.

Your organization has completed its data inventory and data retention policy has been compiled to overlay the data within the organization's possession.

As outlined in the GDPR, data destruction — designated as the elimination, erasure or clearing of digital content — is classified as a form of data processing. It also means any destruction procedures should follow the specific rules set forth by the regulation. Here are three steps that need to be followed:

Step 1: Step one is obviously to implement the appropriate controls allowing data owners full rights and permissions over their affected content. Companies must provide users with an option to delete all personal data — including sales or browsing histories. It absolutely must be a practical option that stems the flow of new content and eliminates the old as soon as possible.

Step 2: Businesses are also obligated to ensure old data or content is securely erased. Just deleting it via the operating system or server is not enough. In fact, reformatting old drives and magnetic media — including hard drives or audio tapes — is no guarantee, either. Deleted data can often be recovered provided the physical media is available.

Step 3: It's important to properly dispose of?

Answers:

A. Hardware
B. Software
C. Records
D. Cloud storage

The correct answer is A. It's important to properly dispose of the hardware involved, too — not just the digital forms of content. One must employ permanent erasure solutions, such as degaussing, which involves the application of magnetic tape to render devices unreadable or unusable. Physical media may also be shredded, crushed, or incinerated to ensure full compliance.

CDPSE: FOCUSED PREPARATION

Question 110.

This technology is a decentralized data structure where the data is distributed across all computers or nodes within a network and every node in the network stores a copy of the ledger.
There is no central administration of the data and the data are agreed upon by consensus by all nodes in the network.
This technology leverages decentralized peer-to-peer computing, cryptography and related technology to verify and propagate a chain of transaction records across a consortium, alliance, partnership, or coalition.

What technology is this?

Answers:

A. Blockchain technology
B. Distributed ledger technology
C. Server technology
D. Internet of Things technology

The correct answer is B. DLT is the most widely recognized implementation through blockchain.

CDPSE: FOCUSED PREPARATION

Question 111.

The National Institute of Standards and Technology (NIST) defines this as "tamper evident and tamper resistant digital ledgers implemented in a distributed fashion (i.e., without a central repository) and usually without a central authority ([e.g.,] a bank, company, or government).

At [its] basic level, it enable[s] a community of users to record transactions in a shared ledger within that community, such that under normal operation of the network no transaction can be changed once published."

What is this?

Answers:

A. Blockchain
B. DLT
C. Cryptography
D. Cryptocurrency

The correct answer is A. DLT is a component that utilizes blockchain, therefore, Answer B is incorrect.

Answer C is the process in which information is turned into letters and numbers to be rendered unreadable by unauthorized persons. Providers are required by HIPAA to use encryption as a means of protection for their patients' ePHI.

Answer D is a digital or virtual currency that uses cryptography and is difficult to counterfeit because of this security feature.

CDPSE: FOCUSED PREPARATION

Question 112.

IT systems form the backbone of every organization, including all financial firms.

Client data continually passes through multiple IT applications and these firms need to understand all data flows across their various systems. The increased trend towards outsourcing development and support functions means that personal client data is often accessed by external vendors, thus significantly increasing the data's net exposure.

Under GDPR, vendors cannot disassociate themselves from obligations towards data access. Similarly, non-EU organizations working in collaboration with EU banks or serving EU citizens need to ensure vigilance while sharing data across borders. GDPR in effect imposes end-to-end accountability to ensure client data stays well protected by enforcing not only the bank, but all its support functions to embrace compliance.

What management program would this best fall under within your governance program?

Answers:

A. Vendor management
B. Risk management
C. Supply chain contingency plan
D. Governance program

The correct answer is A. Vendor management, to include vendor risk assessments is becoming a critical, operational factor in protecting your organization.

CDPSE: FOCUSED PREPARATION

Question 113.

This process ensures that the organization understands, inventories, maps, and controls its data, as it is created and modified through business processes throughout the data lifecycle, from creation or acquisition to retirement.

What is this called?

Answers:

A. Storage
B. Data lifecycle management
C. Creation
D. Destruction

The correct answer is B. Answers A, C, and D are all phases within data lifecycle management.

CDPSE: FOCUSED PREPARATION

Question 114.

All of the following are phases within this management process.
Create, Store, Use, Share, Archive, and Destroy.

What process is this?

Answers:

A. Data Retention Management
B. Records Management
C. Policy Management
D. Data Lifecycle Management

The correct answer is D.

CDPSE: FOCUSED PREPARATION

Question 115.

This principle in healthcare allows for the accessible and actionable exchange of clinical information — including the insights extracted from EHR, medical imaging systems, and other sources — among providers to streamline patient care.

What is this called?

Answers:

A. Vendor Management
B. Business Associate
C. Interconnectivity
D. ACE

The correct answer is C.

CDPSE: FOCUSED PREPARATION

Question 116.

This trust model makes sure that multinational organizations can monitor all attempts at exploiting the vulnerabilities inherent in these web applications and connections.

It can help these organizations provision access in a more effective manner by focusing on data, workloads and identity.

What trust model is this?

Answers:

A. Direct trust
B. Transitive trust
C. Zero trust
D. Assumptive trust

The correct answer is C.

CDPSE: FOCUSED PREPARATION

Question 117.

This technology is comprised of interconnected medical devices and applications that collect data, which is then provided to healthcare IT systems through online computer networks.

For example, smart beds, wearable medical devices, infusion pumps, and embedded devices are all new technologies in this category. These devices present major benefits to providers and patients such as improved drug management, process automation, and enhanced data analytics across multiple domains, improved patient outcomes, and remote patient monitoring.

What is this technology?

Answers:

A. Internet of Things
B. Internet of Medical Things
C. Internet
D. Zero Trust

The correct answer is B. IomT is a subcomponent under IoT's but is focused on medical and healthcare technologies.

The other answers are all distractors.

CDPSE: FOCUSED PREPARATION

Question 118.

This control is about enforcing rules to ensure that only authorized users get access to resources in a system. In healthcare systems this means protecting patient privacy.

This control may be in the physical, administrative, or technical control families.

What control is this?

Answer:

A. HR controls
B. Configuration Management controls
C. Awareness and Training controls
D. Access controls

The correct answer is D. A set of procedures and/or processes, normally automated, which allows access to a controlled area or to information to be controlled, in accordance with pre-established policies and rules.

Answer B is a collection of activities focused on establishing and maintaining the integrity of products and systems, through control of the processes for initializing, changing, and monitoring the configurations of those products and systems throughout the system development life cycle.

Answer C is (1) awareness programs which set the stage for training by changing organizational attitudes to realize the importance of security and the adverse consequences of its failure, (2) training which teaches people the skills that will enable them to perform their jobs more effectively, and (3) education which is targeted for IT security professionals and focuses on developing the ability and vision to perform complex, multi-disciplinary activities.

CDPSE: FOCUSED PREPARATION

Question 119.

This is an authentication system that requires more than one distinct authentication factor for successful authentication. This can be performed using an authenticator or by a combination of authenticators that provide different factors. The three authentication factors are something you know, something you have, and something you are.

What type of authentication is this?

Answers:

A. Single-factor authentication
B. Dual authorization
C. Multi-factor authentication
D. Authentication

The correct answer is C.

Answer A is a characteristic of an authentication system or an authenticator that requires only one authentication factor (something you know, something you have, or something you are) for successful authentication.

Answer B is the system of storage and handling designed to prohibit individual access to certain resources by requiring the presence and actions of at least two authorized persons, each capable of detecting incorrect or unauthorized security procedures with respect to the task being performed.

Answer D is a distractor and incorrect.

CDPSE: FOCUSED PREPARATION

Question 120.

Your medical staff has access to all EMRs. Each staff member is trained frequently on proper handling, access, and protecting of sensitive data. If one of your medical practitioners is unable to access an EMR, and is authorized to access it, which basic security principle has been applied?

Answers:

A. Role-Based Access
B. Segregation of duties
C. Least privilege
D. Need-to-know access

The correct answer is C. Least privilege access grants access to information or systems at the lowest level possible to perform their roles and responsibilities. In this scenario, the medical practitioner has not been provided access to the patient's record, therefore, must request it, based on least privilege access being applied.

CDPSE: FOCUSED PREPARATION

Question 121.

A fundamental part of securing your organization's information is knowing what data you have and who can access it. It's the process of identifying and assigning predetermined levels of sensitivity to different types of information.

This not only means understanding what types of data you own, but what you're doing with it. For example, your organization is a financial institution which holds a person's mortgage application, which contains a wealth of Non-Public Personal Information (NPPI) like income level, current home address, their previous home address, other loan information, and more.

This information needs to be protected. However, the level of protection that is applied depends on the?

Answers:

A. Privacy Policy
B. Data classification it is assigned
C. Technical controls applied
D. Role-Based Access applied

The correct answer is B. Data classification applies and helps your organization properly protect your data based on that classification.

CDPSE: FOCUSED PREPARATION

Question 122.

Your medical staff has access to all EMRs. Each staff member is trained frequently on proper handling, access, and protecting of sensitive data. If one of your medical practitioners accesses an EMR in which they did not and will not provide care to, which basic security principle has been violated?

Answers:

A. Role-Based Access
B. Segregation of duties
C. Least privilege
D. Need-to-know access

The correct answer is D. Need-to-know access is access to information or systems that are required to conduct and complete the responsibility of an authorized user. In this scenario, the medical practitioner is not and will not provide care to the patient, therefore, has no need-to-know to access the patient's records.

CDPSE: FOCUSED PREPARATION

Question 123.

Your organization processes and collects over 1,000,000 credit card transactions annually.

You have conducted an assessment on your PCI-DSS compliance. Prior to finalizing your report of compliance (ROC), you suffer a data breach and identify that your organization did not report nor respond to the breach in an adequate time frame.

What control might not be implemented within your program?

Answers:

A. Phishing training
B. Special handling training
C. Information security
D. Incident response plan

The correct answer is D. Requirement 12.10 of the PCI-DSS states that an organization will "Implement an incident response plan. Be prepared to respond immediately to a system breach". Based on the actual question, answer D is the best, correct answer.

CDPSE: FOCUSED PREPARATION

Question 124.

With COVID-19 still upon us and a number of organizations continuing to work-from-home, remote access for both internal and external sources has increased over the past year.

Remote Desktop Protocol (RDP), the Microsoft Windows component that makes it easy for your employees to connect to work or home computers while they are away, is used by millions.

While RDP operates on an encrypted channel on servers, there is a vulnerability in the encryption method in earlier versions of RDP, making it a preferred gateway by hackers.

For companies that not only want to meet compliance standards but exceed them, RDP security is a challenge. While RDP is built into Microsoft operating systems, it can also be installed on Apple, Linux, and Android operating systems.

Without properly securing it, your RDP can become the gateway where a malware infection or targeted ransomware is deployed, resulting in critical service disruption.

What is the first step in defending against RDP security risks?

Answers:

A. Block TCP port 3389
B. Enabling Network Level Authentication (NLA)
C. Creating a policy to handle endpoints ensuring the port isn't accessible to the internet
D. Limit RDP remote users

The correct answer is C. Best-practice protocol to prevent exposure to RDP security issues starts with creating a policy to handle endpoints and making sure the port isn't accessible to the internet. A proactive approach can help you focus on preventing initial access by minimizing RDP security risks.

Next steps would be to:
- Limit RDP remote users
- Utilize a VPN
- Use a Remote Desktop Gateway in conjunction with the VPN

CDPSE: FOCUSED PREPARATION

Question 125.

It is Monday morning, and you are starting a new role as the privacy solutions engineer.

You log into your corporate email account and find an email from HR. As you read through the email, you see that you are required to complete specific privacy training. What type of control is this?

Answers:

A. Special Handling
B. Data Classification
C. Technical
D. Role-Based Access

The correct answer is D. You are starting a new role; you are being required to complete 'specific' privacy training. Answer A, B, and C will support Role-Based Access controls, but are not the correct answers here.

CDPSE: FOCUSED PREPARATION

Question 126.

This is a crucial part of developing any web or mobile application. It is the combination of programming languages and software underneath a development project.

This, also called a technology infrastructure, or a data ecosystem, is a list of all the technology services used to build and run one single application.

A social media platform may be composed of a combination of coding frameworks and languages including JavaScript, HTML, CSS, PHP, and ReactJS.

What is this called?

Answers:

A. PaaS
B. Technology stack
C. CaaS
D. Infrastructure inventory

The correct answer is B. is defined as the set of technologies an organization uses to build a web or mobile application. It is a combination of programming languages, frameworks, libraries, patterns, servers, UI/UX solutions, software, and tools used by its developers.

CDPSE: FOCUSED PREPARATION

Question 127.

Your organization provides time-sensitive and business sensitive documents and information to your customer, allowing their users to interact with the application in a web browser to upload and interact with both your files and theirs, but all of the data processing and storage happens remotely on the cloud.

What is the name of this type of service?

Answers:

A. Content management system
B. Cloud-as-a-Services
C. Platform-as-a-Service
D. Software-as-a-Service

The correct answer is A. A CMS provides data storage and related automated processes for enterprises to monitor text, images, video, audio or other multimedia content throughout the digital content lifecycle – this includes everything from creation, organization and storage to editing, publishing, archiving or deletion. It also provides individuals and businesses to edit, manage, and maintain existing website pages in a single interface without needing specialized technical knowledge.

CDPSE: FOCUSED PREPARATION

Question 128.

A requirement consisting of locking down all systems within an organization that is capable of obtaining internal access to resources forces privacy solution professionals to look at every possible access route that may be exploited in launching an attack falls into this type of security control

These systems are the most vulnerable components of your computing environment. Implementing these systems and devices with anti-virus software, multi-factor authentication, and automated application updates are simple protections that supplement your organization in securing both yours and any customers or client's data.

What type of security is this?

Answers:

A. Cloud security
B. Remote access
C. Endpoint protection
D. System security

The correct answer is C. Endpoint protection is the practice of securing endpoints or entry points of end-user devices from being exploited by malicious actors and campaigns. Endpoint security systems protect these endpoints on a network or in the cloud from cybersecurity threats.

CDPSE: FOCUSED PREPARATION

Question 129.

What type of data is not considered to be personal data by the GDPR, as detailed in Article 4(1), and its collection and processing is governed by the GDPR. Article 3(2) states that, "This Regulation applies to the processing of personal data of data subjects who are in the Union."

Answers:

A. Geolocation
B. Online identifier
C. Economic
D. Historic

The correct answer is D. Art. 4(1) - 'personal data' means any information relating to an identified or identifiable natural person ('data subject'); an identifiable natural person is one who can be identified, directly or indirectly, in particular by reference to an identifier such as a name, an identification number, location data, an online identifier or to one or more factors specific to the physical, physiological, genetic, mental, economic, cultural or social identity of that natural person.

CDPSE: FOCUSED PREPARATION

Question 130.

In 1996, the Department of Health and Human Services within the United States of America, signed into law the Healthcare Insurance Portability and Accountability Act (HIPAA). HIPAA was created to "improve the portability and accountability of health insurance coverage" for employees between jobs.

Within GDPR, Art. 20 empowers the data subject to have the right receive the personal data concerning him or her, which he or she has provided to a controller, in a structured, commonly used and machine-readable format and have the right to transmit those data to another controller without hindrance from the controller to which the personal data have been provided. This right is what?

Answers:

A. Access
B. Rectification
C. Data portability
D. Automated decision making

The correct answer is C. Recital 68 also addresses the right of data portability. The right to data portability allows data subjects to obtain and reuse personal data about them for their own purposes across different services. It allows data subjects to move, copy or transfer personal data easily from one IT environment to another in a safe and secure way without affecting its usability. This enables data subjects to take advantage of different applications and services that can use their data to find them a better deal or help them understand their spending habits.
The right only applies to information about a data subject provided to a controller.

CDPSE: FOCUSED PREPARATION

Question 131.

As your organization decides on what data to collect, it must identify valid business purposes, known as a lawful basis, for collecting and using personal data. Art. 5(1) of the GDPR outlines six data protection principles. Which is the first?

Answers:

A. Purpose limitation
B. Data minimization
C. Accuracy
D. Fairness

The correct answer is D. The first principle concerns lawfulness, fairness and transparency. It requires that personal data are processed in a lawful, fair and transparent manner in relation to data subjects. Transparency implies that any information and communication concerning the processing of personal data must be easily accessible and easy to understand. Also, clear and plain language needs to be used in this regard. More specifically, this principle ensures data subjects receive information on the identity of controllers and purposes of the processing of personal data.

The second principle is that of purpose limitation.

As the third principle, we need to refer to data minimization.

Accuracy is the fourth principle meaning that it is required to ensure that personal data are accurate and are kept up to date where it is necessary.

The fifth principle is storage limitation.

Finally, the sixth principle of integrity and confidentiality requires that in the processing of personal data appropriate security of personal data is ensured.

In addition to the six data protection principles, the GDPR introduces in Article 5(2) GDPR the principle of accountability, without which they cannot be brought to life. According to this principle, the controller shall be responsible for compliance with the principles listed in Article 5(1) GDPR and addressed above and shall be able to demonstrate its compliance with them.

CDPSE: FOCUSED PREPARATION

Question 132.

GDPR non-compliant fines are based on the specific articles of the Regulation that the organization has breached. Infringements of the organization's obligations, including data security breaches, will be subject to the lower level, whereas infringements of an individual's privacy rights will be subject to the higher level. Data controllers and processors face administrative fines of the higher of €10 million or 2% of annual global turnover for infringements of articles:
8 (conditions for children's consent),
11 (processing that doesn't require identification),
25-39 (general obligations of processors and controllers),
42 (certification), and
43 (certification bodies)

The higher of €20 million or 4% of annual global turnover for infringements of articles:
5 (data processing principles),
6 (lawful bases for processing),
7 (conditions for consent),
9 (processing of special categories of data),
12-22 (data subjects' rights), and
44-49 (data transfers to third countries).

In 2019, British Airways was fined what amount for a 2018 data breach over data security failings which enabled unauthorized access to be obtained to personal and payment card information relating to more than 500,000 of its customers.

Answers:

A. €10 million
B. €20 million
C. €183 million
D. €30 million

The correct answer is C. The $230 million fine (£183.4 million) is 1.5% of BA's global turnover for the year, its parent company International Airlines Group noted in a statement. Under GDPR, companies can be fined the equivalent of $22.4 million or 4% of their total annual worldwide revenue in the preceding financial year, whichever is higher.

CDPSE: FOCUSED PREPARATION

Question 133.

Your organization has implemented a new encryption solution for your stored data.
If your encryption keys become compromised, an unauthorized user may use those keys to:

- Create phishing websites impersonating your original website;
- Pass through your corporate networks by impersonating you or your employees;
- Sign applications or documents in your name;
- Extract/tamper with the data stored on the server; and/or
- Read your encrypted emails and do any number of nefarious things.

If a cyber perpetrator has your keys, they can do any — or all — of that to their benefit and your detriment. They can use your keys to make money by asking for ransom, sell your data to your competitors, go share them on public platforms and ruin your reputation.

No organization wants any of that to happen. That's why encryption key management should be one of your top priorities as far as data security and privacy is concerned.

What NIST standard would you consult for assistance in developing a key management program?

Answers:

A. NIST Special Publication 800-57 part 1, rev. 5
B. NIST Special Publication 800-63 rev. 4
C. NIST Special Publication 800-171 rev. 2
D. NIST Special Publication 800-39

The correct answer is A. The National Institute of Standards and Technology (NIST) put it best in its Special Publication 800-57 part 1, rev. 5:

"Cryptographic keys play an important part in the operation of cryptography. These keys are analogous to the combination of a safe. If a safe combination is known to an adversary, the strongest safe provides no security against penetration. The proper management of cryptographic keys is essential to the effective use of cryptography for security. Poor key management may easily compromise strong algorithms."

CDPSE: FOCUSED PREPARATION

Question 134.

You are the privacy solutions engineer within your organization. Your organization processes personal data wholly or partly by automated means and the processing other than by automated means of personal data which do form part of a filing system or are intended to form a filing system applies to which GDPR article?

Answers:

A. Art. 2
B. Art. 3
C. Art. 1
D. Art. 4

The correct answer is A. Article 2 addresses Material scope.

Answer B, Article 3, addresses Territorial scope and the processing of personal data in the context of the activities of an establishment of a controller or a processor in the Union, regardless of whether the processing takes place in the Union or not.
This Regulation applies to the processing of personal data of data subjects who are in the Union by a controller or processor not established in the Union, where the processing activities are related to: the offering of goods or services, irrespective of whether a payment of the data subject is required, to such data subjects in the Union; or the monitoring of their behavior as far as their behavior takes place within the Union.
This Regulation applies to the processing of personal data by a controller not established in the Union, but in a place where Member State law applies by virtue of public international law.
Answer C addresses Subject-matter and objectives while Answer D addresses Definitions.

CDPSE: FOCUSED PREPARATION

Question 135.

You are the privacy solutions engineer within your organization. Your organization processes personal data of data subjects who are in the Union by a controller or processor not established in the Union, where the processing activities are related to the offering of goods or services. Which GDPR article applies?

Answers:

A. Art. 2
B. Art. 3
C. Art. 1
D. Art. 4

The correct answer is B. Article 3 addresses Territorial scope and the processing of personal data in the context of the activities of an establishment of a controller or a processor in the Union, regardless of whether the processing takes place in the Union or not.
This Regulation applies to the processing of personal data of data subjects who are in the Union by a controller or processor not established in the Union, where the processing activities are related to: the offering of goods or services, irrespective of whether a payment of the data subject is required, to such data subjects in the Union; or the monitoring of their behavior as far as their behavior takes place within the Union.
This Regulation applies to the processing of personal data by a controller not established in the Union, but in a place where Member State law applies by virtue of public international law.
Answer C addresses Subject-matter and objectives while Answer D addresses Definitions.

CDPSE: FOCUSED PREPARATION

Question 136.

Your organization completed the data inventory exercise. What term is explicitly highlighted in Article 6(4)(e) as an "appropriate safeguard" that can be used by data controllers "in order to ascertain whether processing for another purpose is compatible with the purpose for which the personal data are initially collected?

Answers:

A. Data minimization
B. Anonymize
C. Pseudonymization
D. Data encryption

The correct answer is C. Recital 28, Introduction of Pseudonymization, states that the application of pseudonymization to personal data can reduce the risks to the data subjects concerned and help controllers and processors to meet their data-protection obligations. The explicit introduction of 'pseudonymization' in this Regulation is not intended to preclude any other measures of data protection.

CDPSE: FOCUSED PREPARATION

Question 137.

Which data protection principle entails that personal data must be kept in a form that makes it possible to identify data subjects for no longer than is necessary for the purposes of the processing. Keeping these data for longer periods is allowed when the processing of the data will aim at achieving purposes in the public interest, scientific or historical research purposes or statistical purposes. Nevertheless, also in these cases rights and freedoms of data subjects must be safeguarded.

Answers:

A. Purpose limitation
B. Storage
C. Integrity and Confidentiality
D. Accuracy

The correct answer is B. The fifth principle is storage limitation. It entails that personal data must be kept in a form that makes it possible to identify data subjects for no longer than is necessary for the purposes of the processing. Storing these data for longer periods is allowed when the processing of the data will aim at achieving purposes in the public interest, scientific or historical research purposes or statistical purposes. Nevertheless, also in these cases rights and freedoms of data subjects must be safeguarded.

CDPSE: FOCUSED PREPARATION

Question 138.

What does a trusted platform module utilized to secure both a key and software on a system provide your organization?

Answers:

A. Speeds up the encryption process utilizing the system bus
B. Guarantees confidentiality of the system data
C. Secures data until other conditions are met
D. Ensures the encryption key will never be utilized outside of its system

The correct answer is A. Trusted Platform Module (TPM) technology is designed to provide hardware-based, security-related functions. A TPM chip is a secure crypto-processor that is designed to carry out cryptographic operations.

The most common TPM functions are used for system integrity measurements and for key creation and use. During the boot process of a system, the boot code that is loaded (including firmware and the operating system components) can be measured and recorded in the TPM.

CDPSE: FOCUSED PREPARATION

Question 139.

While in the maintenance stage within the System Development Life Cycle (SDLC), a vulnerability is discovered.

What actions must be taken?

Answers:

A. Report the vulnerability
B. Make changes following the guidelines
C. Stop the application development and mitigate the vulnerability
D. Monitor the application and review code

The correct answer is B. Once the application is in production, you follow and adhere to the principle and design guidelines and investigate the vulnerability and develop a mitigation plan for the vulnerability.

CDPSE: FOCUSED PREPARATION

Question 140.

Your organization is working on implementing and protecting the contact tracing applications that it utilizes. You have built application programming interfaces (API) and other applications to support this project.

A few questions you have been asking and documenting answers provided are to what data is being collected and who is this data being shared with.

You compile your final report and highlight a few of the risks identified that your organization must address.

Which of the following are not risks associated with tracking technologies?

Answers:

A. Geo-location tracking
B. Beacon-based tracking
C. Online behavioral tracking
D. Financial expense tracking

The correct answer is D. The other three answers are all risks associated with tracking technologies.

CDPSE: FOCUSED PREPARATION

Question 141.

You, the privacy solutions engineer for your organization, is designing processes and procedures for protecting applications from being reverse engineered back to its source code and from bad actors inspecting internal values, monitoring or tampering with the application.

What type of security controls are you executing?

Answers:

A. Software hardening
B. Secure Development Lifecycle
C. Application hardening
D. System hardening

The correct answer is C. Application hardening is an integral part of the defense strategy for businesses intent on building a trusted mobile environment with a secure software development lifecycle process.

CDPSE: FOCUSED PREPARATION

Question 142.

In order for data classification to work, the data should meet some criteria that enable a decision to be made about what classification applies.
The presence of one of the following two capabilities should be applied.
-An automated system that can analyze the data and apply rules to make that decision
-An interface for users to create, verify or override a classification.
-Discovery in a variety of data storage environments is a key capability for automated systems.
-The provision of a recording of that classification that allows other systems and processes to leverage that decision.
-The inclusion of a log, dashboard or other method to allow data and security administrators to understand the data estate for a variety of reasons.

Where does the data classification program add value to?

Answers:

A. Information Asset Identification
B. Asset Valuation
C. Risk Assessment
D. Risk Management

The correct answer is B. Data classification entails analyzing the data that the organization collects and uses or shares, assessing the criticality and value of the data (asset), and then assigning it to a category.

Asset value is an item perceived as having value. Answer A is a sub-component of identifying what assets/information you have, and you must complete that task prior to applying a classification to the asset/information.

Answers C and D are not correct.

CDPSE: FOCUSED PREPARATION

Question 143.

You are consulting with your information security team on new lifecycle processes.
You are promoting the incorporation of data protection via their technology designs and infrastructure implementations.
You remember that you can have security without privacy, however, you cannot have privacy without security.
What design model is this referencing?

Answers:

A. Privacy by Default
B. Privacy by Design
C. Integrity and Confidentiality
D. Privacy Program

The correct answer is B. Privacy by design or data protection by design is when your organization is developing, designing, selecting and using applications, services and products that are based on the processing of personal data or process personal data to fulfil their task, producers of the products, services and applications should be encouraged to take into account the right to data protection when developing and designing such products, services and applications and, with due regard to the state of the art, to make sure that controllers and processors are able to fulfil their data protection obligations.

Answer A, Privacy by Default, is the implementation of appropriate technical and organizational measures for ensuring that, by default, only personal data which are necessary for each specific purpose of the processing are processed.

Answer C is one of the six data processing principles.

CDPSE: FOCUSED PREPARATION

Question 144.

You are the new risk management professional in an international organization.

You have applied your asset valuation exercise to your most critical assets across the globe and are in the process of gathering new global threats and vulnerabilities applicable to your organization.

When reviewing the current risk management framework, you determine that it may not be as robust and focused on international risk management.

Which of the following frameworks might better suit your organization?

Answers:

A. ISO 27005:2018
B. ISO 31000:2018
C. ISO 27799:2016
D. NIST SP 800-53Rev4

The correct answer is B. ISO 31000:2018 is an international risk management framework created to support an international organization.

Answers A and C are geared towards information security risk management and the question does not ask for information security risk management information.

CDPSE: FOCUSED PREPARATION

Question 145.

Asymmetric algorithms are utilized for which of the following when using SSL/TLS for implementing network security?

Answers:

A. Encryption
B. Session encryption
C. Peer encryption
D. Payload data encryption

The correct answer is D. Payload encryption is an engineering pattern providing granular control over content encryption.

CDPSE: FOCUSED PREPARATION

Question 146.

Which of the following risk management lifecycle processes is where the implemented control is verified for the effectiveness based on the stated control objectives?

Answers:

A. Plan
B. Do
C. Check
D. Act

The correct answer is C. The risk management lifecycle follows the PLAN, DO, CHECK, ACT model with PLAN=Identifying and analyzing risk; DO=Creating a mitigation plan; CHECK=Implement controls; and ACT=Monitor.

Checking will assess the effectiveness of the implemented controls against the control objectives to determine if they are producing the required results.

CDPSE: FOCUSED PREPARATION

Question 147.

On July 16, 2020, the CJEU invalidated the E.U.-U.S. Privacy Shield, one of the methods for transfers of personal data into the U.S. The court found that under U.S. surveillance laws, the U.S. government has access to personal data that does not provide Europeans with privacy protections equivalent to those in the E.U.
Which answer below is most associated with this ruling?

Answers:

A. Schrems
B. Snowden
C. GDRP
D. Privacy Protection

The correct answer is A. One of the most important international privacy cases in recent history arose from a complaint against Facebook brought to the Irish Data Protection Commissioner by an Austrian privacy advocate named Max Schrems. In the complaint, Mr. Schrems challenged the transfer of his data (and the data of EU citizens' generally) to the United States by Facebook, which is incorporated in Ireland. The case ("Schrems I") led the Court of Justice of the European Union on October 6, 2015, to invalidate the Safe Harbor arrangement, which governed data transfers between the EU and the US.

Answer B is incorrect. Edward Snowden is an American whistleblower who copied and leaked highly classified information from the National Security Agency (NSA) in 2013 when he was a Central Intelligence Agency (CIA) employee and subcontractor. His disclosures revealed numerous global surveillance programs, many run by the NSA and the Five Eyes Intelligence Alliance with the cooperation of telecommunication companies and European governments and prompted a cultural discussion about national security and individual privacy.

CDPSE: FOCUSED PREPARATION

Question 148.

Your organization is developing its data storage strategy and incorporating security, privacy, costs, analytics and more.

All of the following are critical risks to the data except?

Answers:

A. Incompetent analytics
B. Data destruction
C. Cost management
D. Data gravity

The correct answer is D. Data migration is the process of moving data from one location to another, one format to another, or one application to another. Data gravity, a part of data migration describes how data attracts other data to it as it grows, how it is integrated into production and how it becomes customized over time.

The other answers are all critical risks within the strategy of data storage, while data gravity would be a risk for operations at a tactical level of risk.

CDPSE: FOCUSED PREPARATION

Question 149.

As your organization researches best practices for data destruction, it reviews all of the data and medium's its data resides on.

What is the best practice?

Answers:

A. Physical destruction
B. Degaussing
C. Overwriting
D. Deleting

The correct answer to the question is A. The key word in the question is data destruction.

Answer B does not provide a way to ensure all data is destroyed. The process renders the drive inoperable and unverifiable. Additionally, degaussing does not eradicate data from non-magnetic media such as SSDs and CDs.

Answer C writes new data on top of the old data, leaving remanence of the old data.

Answer D is a distractor.

CDPSE: FOCUSED PREPARATION

Question 150.

De-identification and anonymization are strategies that are used to remove patient identifiers in electronic health record (EHR) data. The use of these strategies in multicenter research studies is paramount in importance, given the need to share EHR data across multiple environments and institutions while safeguarding patient privacy.

What method is best for de-identification of data?

Answers:

A. Encryption
B. Pseudonymization
C. Removal of specified individual identifiers
D. Anonymization

The correct answer is C.

Answer A does not de-identify data. It protects it.

Answer B and D, with anonymization, the data is scrubbed for any information that may serve as an identifier of a data subject. Pseudonymization does not remove all identifying information from the data but merely reduces the linkage of a dataset with the original identity of an individual (e.g., via an encryption scheme).

CDPSE: FOCUSED PREPARATION

Answer Key:

1. D	41. C	81. C
2. D	42. A	82. A
3. D	43. A	83. D
4. C	44. B	84. B
5. A	45. C	85. A
6. B	46. B	86. C
7. D	47. B	87. B
8. B	48. B	88. C
9. A	49. C	89. D
10. C	50. C	90. D
11. D	51. D	91. A
12. D	52. C	92. D
13. B	53. A	93. C
14. D	54. D	94. B
15. C	55. A	95. D
16. C	56. B	96. B
17. B	57. C	97. C
18. C	58. A	98. C
19. D	59. B	99. D
20. D	60. A	100. A
21. D	61. D	101. C
22. D	62. D	102. C
23. B	63. D	103. B
24. A	64. B	104. C
25. D	65. D	105. A
26. C	66. D	106. B
27. C	67. D	107. A
28. B	68. B	108. D
29. D	69. C	109. A
30. B	70. B	110. B
31. C	71. D	111. A
32. D	72. C	112. A
33. C	73. D	113. B
34. A	74. D	114. D
35. D	75. A	115. C
36. A	76. D	116. C
37. C	77. C	117. B
38. B	78. D	118. D
39. A	79. B	119. C
40. C	80. C	120. C

CDPSE: FOCUSED PREPARATION

Answer Key (cont):

121. B
122. D
123. D
124. C
125. D
126. B
127. A
128. C
129. D
130. C
131. D
132. C
133. A
134. A
135. B
136. C
137. B
138. A
139. B
140. D
141. C
142. B
143. B
144. B
145. D
146. C
147. A
148. D
149. A
150. C

www.ingramcontent.com/pod-product-compliance
Lightning Source LLC
Chambersburg PA
CBHW070616220526
45466CB00001B/24